THE RETAIL INVESTOR

3 Books in 1 - Invest Masterfully and Achieve Financial Freedom

Big Jodhi

Kristen Kiong

Disclaimer:

Investing and starting any kind of business (physical or online) involves substantial risk. Please do not misinterpret content in this book as a financial recommendation to buy/sell any securities, or to throw your life's savings into any form of business venture. Content provided in this book are for informational purposes only. The author does not make any guarantee as to any results that may be obtained from its content.

While information in this book is believed to be reliable, the author does not warrant completeness and accuracy of the content discussed in this book, and the author specifically disclaims any responsibility for any liability, loss, or risk, personal or otherwise, which is incurred as a consequence, directly or indirectly, of the use and application of any contents of this book.

Do your own research and seek advice from a professional financial advisor before dabbling into any form of investments or business ventures. You can lose all your invested capital if you are not careful. The author will not be liable for any losses or damages resulting from the material and content from this book.

Information presented on this book is not guaranteed as accurate. This book provides historical data to discuss and illustrate underlying principles, past data does not guarantee future results. Performance data changes over time, the author shall not be responsible for updating or correcting any information or opinion herein.

Cover design by: Kristen Kiong
Printed in the United States of America

CONTENTS

INTRODUCTION: HOW TO ANALYSE BUSINESSES IN THE STOCK MARKET

Welcome to the world of stock picking and investing. Capitalism forever! I hope that this book gives you an insight on the beginnings and basics of the stock market investing. It is imperative that as an individual, whatever vocation you are in, to understand financial markets because everyone needs money, and everyone needs to know how to save and grow their money. People always complain that the capitalist pigs do not care about the laymen, and that the rich get richer. I beg to differ. In fact, we have always had the same opportunity to be wealthy, we just need to have the burning desire to be curious and find out more about how to get wealthy! We have the sole responsibility to take charge of our own lives and learn; if we just believe that ignorance is bliss, you are in for a rude shock, maybe not now, but 10-20 years from now. Ignorance is not bliss, in fact, ignorance is poverty, and poverty stinks! You hear me?!

We will use a fictional cake business, named Great Cakes, to illustrate all the investing concepts discussed in this book. Enjoy!

CHAPTER 1

The Stock Market

"Let your money work for you", I bet many of you hear that a lot, it sounds so easy to do, and yet not many actually know, or even bother to find out how to get started. I asked a colleague of mine a question the other day, on whether he thought that he'd ever be a millionaire in his life, and his answer was a very convicted and immediate "no!", almost to a point where he sounded insulted that I even asked. He's in his mid-20s.

To many people, being wealthy seems like a fantasy or a dream that is unachievable unless they somehow catch a big break, you know, like, win the lottery, get promoted with a high paying job, or maybe find crude oil in their backyard. Yet the truth of the matter is , you don't need any of these, in fact , all you need is a little knowledge, some discipline, a heck of a lot of patience, and, the most crucial of all, a burning desire to be wealthy, you would have almost certainly sealed your destiny in the years to come. The destiny of being rich that is. If you've been leaving your money sitting in the bank and have no idea of how to make it grow for you, please read on, I'd like to Invite you to a very special place where your money would be happier. It's called the stock market.

What is a stock market? Ever been to a meat market? What do they sell? Of course, it's meat. So, a stock market sells, well, stocks, but what type of stocks? Stocks of businesses, or rather, ownership shares of businesses. (P.S. stocks and shares are the same thing). The stock market (or a stock exchange) is a place where buyers and sellers come together to trade with each other for ownership shares of businesses. The idea of a stock market is a little like crowdfunding, it supplies businesses with the money they need to meet the growing demand of their products and services. The "funders", or investors, providing the money are big institutions like banks, mutual funds, pension funds and insurance companies, and ordinary people like you and me. How does buying and owning a business stock benefit you, you may ask. Well, businesses earn money, right? when u buy a share of a business, you get a claim on the profits that they earn!

So, in essence, the stock market, or stock exchange, consists of buyers and sellers of business stock. Next, you might be thinking, how did these sellers get their hands on these business stocks in the first place? They couldn't have been cultivating it in a pig farm Somewhere right? Of course not! Stockholders get their stock through a process called an initial public offering (IPO). Before I get down to explaining IPO, I would first like to address how a business comes about.

Let's imagine a hypothetical situation. Say you set up a bakery selling cakes, you name your bakery business "Great Cakes", you design a logo to build some brand image , and you rent a small unit in a shopping centre to run your business. Great Cakes takes off slowly, selling 100 cakes in the first year. Word of mouth spreads and more and more people start hearing about Great Cakes over time. In the second year, Great Cakes sells 200 cakes, you have experienced a double volume in your sales! You are over the moon, but also, you're exhausted from all the work and realise that you need help. So, with the profits that you've earned, you hire a staff and set up a second shop. You have successfully expanded your Business using your own business profits, in other words, your own money to grow your business. Over the next 8 years, because of Great Cakes' phenomenal cakes, you have managed to expand another 8 bakeries! Business is booming and you now own a steady business, however, you notice that there's always a long queue outside your bakery shops. Every day, and a good chunk of these customers never get their orders fulfilled. You do some market research and surveys with your loyal customers and realise that in order to meet the demands of all your customers now, you need another 10 more additional shops with 100 employees to run the shops, all by the following year. You crack your head and ask yourself, "how am I going to get the financial resources to increase another 10 bakeries by next year, I took 10 years to grow to 10 bakeries using all of my profits to grow the business , Where do I get the funding to double my existing business to meet the demands of all my customers?" This is when you decide that Great Cakes needs to go public and get listed on the stock exchange. With the help of an investment banker and several brokers, you finally get Great Cakes listed on the stock exchange and get the funding you require to expand the business further. This is when an IPO comes in handy. An IPO is a process whereby a growing business decides to sell a part of its ownership to the public, ultimately to get the funding they need to meet with the marketplace's growing demand for their products and services. In return, the buyers of the business (who now own parts of the business, or stockholders) would get a cut of the profits that the business makes. Yes guys, it's like a big shark tank. It's really wonderful.

In Great Cakes' case, let's say the business divides itself into 1 million shares, and values itself at 1 dollar a share. Once Great Cakes sells all of its shares to willing buyers in the stock market, Great Cakes would receive a million dollars in cold hard cash (minus investment bankers and Brokers commissions), and use the capital for expansion. This is the function and general process of a stock market, in a nutshell. Now, back to the hypothetical story. It's year 11 for Great Cakes and you have managed to publicly list your company on the stock exchange! You've got just shy of a million dollars in cash, and you start using the money to build more bakeries and hire more staff. Business booms even more, and by the end of year 11 Great cakes made $100,000 in profits. You decide to keep half of the profits into the business for further expansion, and half of it to be distributed in cash to Great Cakes stockholders as dividends. This is where the stockholders get their fun. Half of Great Cakes' profits will be paid out as dividends to stockholders ($50,000), and this $50,000 will be divided equally amongst the 1 million shares, leading to each share entitled to 5 cents of profit ($50k/1 mil shares). Now, if a retail investor had bought 100 shares of Great Cakes, he would get a dividend of $5, and if the business maintains its financial performance (or even improve) in the years to come, there is a high probability that the retail investor can get 5 dollars or more every single year. The yield from the initial investment of $100 of Great Cakes shares (Great Cakes was sold at $1 per share at its IPO) is 5% annually. Banks now pay a usurious rate of less than 1 % interest on savings accounts. If you, my dear reader, had put your savings to work by buying business stocks instead, rather than leaving it parked "safely" in a stinky ol' bank, you would be making more than 5 times the return on your money. Oh, and did I mention, you didn't have to work for it, your money did it for you. It seems, you can actually have your Great Cakes, and eat it!

CHAPTER 2

Three Financial Statements

There are the 3 Financial Statements that you MUST learn to understand if you want to analyse stocks properly - The income statement, the balance sheet and the cashflow statement. In this chapter, you will get a quick overview about the 3 main financial statements found in an annual report, with each financial statement comes very insightful information about the company.

The income statement

This financial statement presents the financial performance of the business for the year; it consists of revenue, cost of goods sold, operating expenses, interest costs, taxes, depreciation, and amortization. Finally, after subtracting all these expenses, it will show the net profit for the year.

The balance sheet

This financial statement shows the financial health of a company, breaking down its assets, liabilities, and owner's equity. Investors need to understand this very well to determine if a company is financially stable or not.

The cashflow statement

This financial statement monitors the movement of cash in the business, the net profit in the income statement does not necessarily reflect the exact amount of residual cash that was collected by the business. One must understand the mechanics behind the cashflow statement, to find the true operating earnings of the company, and how CASH is actually generated from the business itself.

Income statement

Every investor must learn about the income statement of a typical company. In stock investing, we must learn about the prospective company's fundamentals, and we must have a feel of their earnings. So how do we do this? By looking at the income statement of course. To use an analogy, the income statement is like a report card on your exam performance, similarly, the income statement shows the profits made or losses made by the company for the year. Seasoned investors will take past income statements and plot their earnings on a graph, if the line is going upwards, it means that the company's profits and earnings are increasing, and vice versa if it's moving downwards. There are 6 main parts in an income statement.

1. Revenue - this is the total amount of sales generated by the company. The higher the revenue, the higher the market share of the company.

2. Cost of goods sold - this shows the amount of money required to purchase the raw materials needed to make the actual product that the company is selling, and ultimately selling the finished product to collect the revenue for the year.

3. Gross profit - this is the profit gained after just subtracting the Cost of goods sold, we have not

taken into account the operating expenses yet.

4. Operating expenses - these are expenses that are required for running the business. 2 basic examples would be selling and distribution expense, and administrative expense.

5. EBITDA - earnings before interest taxes depreciation amortization. In other words, operating profit.

6. Other expenses - we need to remove the above-mentioned expenses, which would finally lead us to the NET PROFIT or PROFIT FOR THE YEAR. This net profit is like the final grade in your exam. A very important number and it reflects a great deal on the company's ability to generate profits and increase shareholder value.

Let's have a look at Great Cakes' income statement at the end of the fiscal year.

Income Statement

Revenue	**$9,000**
Cost of sales	$3,000
Gross Profit	**$6,000**
Expenses	
Selling and distribution	$500
Administrative	$1,000
EBITDA	**$4,500**
Finance costs	$75
Tax	$45
Depreciation	$1,000
Amortisation	$0
Profit for the year	**$3,380**

The revenue is at the top line. The first value ($9,000) that we see in the income statement, below it is the cost of sales ($3,000). Subtract

$3,000 from $9,000 and we get a gross profit of $6,000. This is not the end. We still need to account for business expenses, reflected further down the rows.

General expenses will include selling, distribution, and administrative expense. Wages will sometimes be included, but for simplicity's sake, I'm going to leave it out. Subtract general expenses off the gross profit, and you get the earnings before interest, tax, depreciation, and amortization. EBITDA. Say it out loud, Eeee – bit – Dah. It's a very common business term and used regularly to measure a business's operating profit.

Now we subtract the final expenses off, which is finance costs, tax, depreciation, and amortization, we get the profit for the year. In other words, Great Cakes' retained earnings.

There you have it! A brief description on a typical income statement. 1 out of 3 financial statements done. Next, we move on to the balance sheet.

Balance sheet

Ever wondered if a company is safe to buy? Where can we find the info on how strong a company is financially? We find this info through their balance sheet. We must learn to read and understand the balance sheet. Period. Imagine you are a doctor looking at an x-ray of a patient, to check if he or she has any irregularities in his or her body. This is exactly what we are doing as investors when we look at the balance sheet. We are looking through the insides of a company to see if the company is healthy or not, financially. Like how a human body has organs, so too does a company, and it is the form of assets, liabilities, and owner's equity. The balance sheet is made up of 3 parts.

Assets - things or items that generate profits/money for the company in one way or another. For example, a piece of machinery is an asset to a company, because it is essential in making finished products for the company/ business to sell.

Liabilities - things or items that take money out of the company. The business/ company is obliged to settle these liabilities at some point in time. Companies always want to take advantage of current market demand, but if they don't have the financial resources to produce more goods and services, they need to borrow money, or take on debt to fund these opportunities. Hence, a debt is a form of liability as it is money owed to a lender and must be paid back at some point in time.

Owner's equity - this is the original seed money that was put into the business in the first place. In simplistic terms, this is the net worth of the company. Retained earnings are also reflected in this segment. The more the owner's equity increases, the more valuable a company will be, ultimately leading to an increase in shareholder value as well. I say again, understanding how to read a balance sheet is crucial in successful stock investing. Learn this well. Let's use a scenario from Great Cakes' business.

Scenario

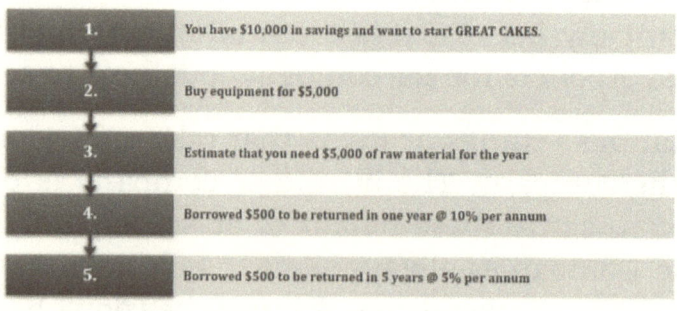

1.	You have $10,000 in savings and want to start GREAT CAKES.
2.	Buy equipment for $5,000
3.	Estimate that you need $5,000 of raw material for the year
4.	Borrowed $500 to be returned in one year @ 10% per annum
5.	Borrowed $500 to be returned in 5 years @ 5% per annum

The image above shows a sequence of events that has happened at the start of Great Cakes. All these events will be reflected in the balance sheet as follows.

Now, before we get into the numbers in the balance sheet, we must understand how the 3 main components assets, liabilities and owner's equity are related to one another. The formula is shown below.

Formula for balance sheet

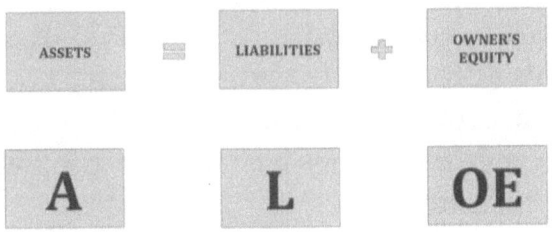

The total amount of assets must always be equal to the sum of liabilities and owner's equity, that is why it is called a balance sheet, the 2 sides must balance. You'll see how it works soon. Let's carry on. First, as in the scenario listed out earlier in step 1, the $10,000 in savings will be in the

Assets column.

Balance sheet at the Start of business

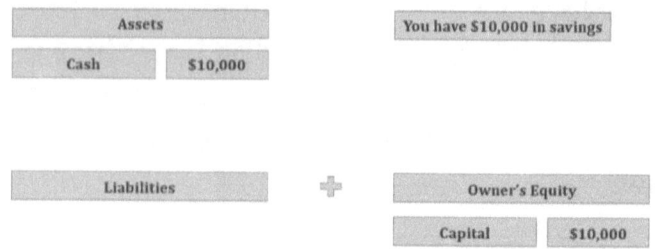

Now that the assets column is $10,000 in value in the cash account, the owner's equity column will open a capital account to reflect that same $10,000. Hence both sides balance (nothing in the liabilities column yet).

Steps 2,3,4 and 5 will then follow suit. All the steps are reflected in the balance sheet.

Balance sheet at Year 0 (The start of GREAT CAKES)

Assets	
Cash	$1,000
Equipment	$5,000
Inventory	$5,000

Liabilities	
Short term debt	$500
Long term debt	$500

Buy equipment for $5,000
Buy raw materials for $5,000
Borrow $500 @ 10%/1 year
Borrow $500 @ 5%/5 years

Owner's Equity	
Capital	$10,000

If you had noticed, the cash account is now down to $1,000 because of the following steps:

Initial cash amount = $10,000

Buying equipment = -$5,000

Buying raw material = -$5,000

Borrowing $500 short term debt = +$500

Borrowing $500 long term debt = +$500

Outstanding cash amount = $(10,000 – 5,000 – 5,000 + 500 + 500) = $1,000

Similarly, since equipment was bought, the equipment value of $5,000 must be reflected in the equipment account, and raw materials will be under the inventory account, also valued at

$5,000. Next, total debt of $1,000 (short term + long term) was incurred, hence the $1,000 is reflected in the liabilities column, $500 short term, and $500 long term. The owner's equity column stays the same. Now, try adding up the assets column, you'll find that the sum is $11,000. Add up the liabilities and owner's equity columns together, and what do you get? $11,000 as well! See how both sides balance? This is how companies reflect their overall value, broken down into the 3 main balance sheet components.

Accounts Receivable

I'm going to throw a curveball now. Remember how $9,000 was reflected as revenue for Great Cakes? Let's assume that out of the $9,000 earned revenue, $500 was paid on credit. The remaining $8,500 was paid in cash. $3,000 of worth of inventory was sold to earn that $9,000 revenue. Let's see how this event is reflected in the balance sheet.

Accounts receivable

Customers who have consumed the cakes but have yet to pay/ used credit and have not given cash yet.

Out of $9,000 Revenue, $500 was paid on credit.

$3,000 worth of inventory was sold (cost of sales).

Assets	
Cash	$9,500
Equipment	$5,000
Inventory	$2,000
Accounts receivable	$500

$8,500 was collected as cash. So we add that $8,500 to our cash balance of $1,000 to make $9,500.

Firstly, we know that Great Cake's latest cash account is $1,000. So, now that $8,500 was collected in cash, we increase the cash account to $9,500 ($1,000 + $8,500). Also, we know that $3,000 of inventory was sold, so we reduce the inventory account to $2,000 ($5,000 - $3,000).

Ok, so with all that settled, what do we do with the remaining $500 paid on credit? We open a new Accounts Receivable account to reflect the $500 credit. The Accounts receivable account reflects the amount of product/ service rendered to customers but have not paid the business in cash yet. These customers would pay at a later date.

Accounts Payable

Curveball #2. Great Cakes decides to buy another $1,000 worth of raw material, but on credit. Let's see how this affects the balance sheet.

Accounts payable
Items that you bought but have not paid up in cash yet.

Additional $1,000 raw materials bought on credit.

Assets			Liabilities	
Cash	$9,500		Short term debt	$500
Equipment	$5,000		Long term debt	$500
Inventory	$3,000		Accounts Payable	$1000
Accounts receivable	$500			

So, when Great Cakes pays on credit, it means that the business will not have to fork out the cash immediately, hence the cash account stays the same at $9,500. However, because new raw material worth $1,000 has been acquired, the inventory account must increase by $1,000 to reflect the total value of all the raw material in Great Cakes, which would ultimately bring the inventory account to $3,000 (the last reflected amount is $2,000, so it will be $2,000 + $1,000).

When Great Cakes pays on credit, the business must open an Accounts Payable account in its liabilities column to reflected money owed. An accounts payable account reflects items that a business has bought but not paid for it in cash yet. In this case, Great Cakes now owes $1,000 to its raw material suppliers, hence the accounts payable account opens up, reflecting the $1,000 owed. Now that we have settled the bulk of the business operations, let's link the income statement to the balance sheet, the final aspect of this exercise.

Bringing in the Income statement

Selling and distribution ($500), administrative ($1000), finance costs ($75), tax ($45), depreciation ($1000).			
Short term debt of $500 was paid off at the end of the year.			
Assets		**Liabilities**	
Cash	$7,380	Short term debt	$0
Equipment	$4,000	Long term debt	$500
Inventory	$3,000	Accounts Payable	$1000
Accounts receivable	$500		

The income statement will generally affect the cash account, as the income statement reflects revenue coming in the business, and expenses going out of the business. The expenses are listed below.

Selling and distribution = - $500

Administrative = - $1,000

Finance costs = -$75

Tax = -$45

Ignore the depreciation expense at this point. It will be explained more in detail at the end of this chapter.

So, add all the expenses up ($500 + $1,000 + $74 + $45 = $1,620), and subtract the sum of expenses from the cash account ($9,500), and you'll get a cash account of $7,880. Now, if you look at the cash account, something's amiss, why is the cash account reflected as $7,380? Curveball #3. Great Cakes decides to settle its short-term loan of $500 since it's due, hence, we subtract $500 out of the cash account, to give a final cash account amount of $7,380. Also, the short-term debt account in the liabilities column will be reduced to zero.

Last step, where do retained earnings for the fiscal year go to? In the Owner's Equity column of course!

Assets		Liabilities	
Non current assets		**Non current Liabilities**	
Equipment	$4,000	Long term debt	$500
Current assets		**Current Liabilities**	
Cash	$7,380	Short term debt	$0
Inventory	$3,000	Accounts Payable	$1,000
Accounts receivable	$500		
Total Assets	$14,880	Total Liabilities	$1500
		Owner's Equity	
		Capital	$10,000
		Retained Earnings	$3,380

The balance sheet must balance!

If you recall, in the income statement, the profit for the year was $3,380. So, we simply add this amount inside the owner's equity column. Remember the $1,000 in depreciation mentioned earlier? We need to subtract it off the equipment account to reduce the value of the equipment (wear and tear of all equipment will occur as time goes by, inevitably reducing the value of the equipment as well). Let's do this check one last time, add up the total assets, and you get $14,880. Add up total liabilities and Owner's equity together, and what do you get? $14,880 as well! Remember, the balance sheet must balance.

And that's it! We're done with all the business operations that happened in Great Cakes' fiscal year. This is what Great Cakes' balance sheet will

look like on a spreadsheet.

GREAT CAKES' Balance Sheet

Assets			Liabilities		
Non current assets			*Non current liabilities*		
Equipment	$	4,000	Long term debt	$	500
Current assets			*Current liabilities*		
Cash	$	7,380	Accounts payable	$	1,000
Inventory	$	3,000			
Accounts Receivable	$	500	**Owner's Equity**		
			Capital	$	10,000
			Retained earnings	$	3,380
Total Assets	$	14,880	**Total liabilities + Owner's Equity**	$	14,880

Please read through this chapter again if all this doesn't make sense to you (I have failed as an author and teacher). Kidding, accounting principles are not easy to grasp, it takes a little bit of practice. So, don't stress yourself out, take your time to digest the concepts discussed here, be patient and continue reading more balance sheets in company annual reports. You'll get the hang of it in due time. Hang in there.

Current vs Non-Current

One more thing. If you have noticed, in the balance sheet, the assets and liabilities are categorised under current and non-current. Current essentially means "in one year" and non-current means "more than 1 year". Let me give you an example of each of them.

So, a current asset is an item that will be settled within a year, meaning that the business will receive cash for it in at most a years' time, for instance, accounts receivable (customers will most likely pay for products within a year, tops). A non-current asset is less liquid, and harder to sell, also, it is highly unlikely that a company would need to sell a non-current asset, as it would most definitely need to use it in some way to run business operations. A warehouse or equipment are some examples of non-current assets.

A current liability is an item that the company needs to pay up for by the end of the year. A good example is the short-term debt of $500 that we discussed about earlier; Great Cakes was obligated to settle the short-term debt within a year, hence that debt was parked under current liabilities. Accounts payable would also often be under the current liabilities column. The business is obligated to pay for these liabilities by the end of the fiscal year, maybe even earlier. A non-current liability is a financial obligation that a company can settle in more than a years' time, for instance, the long-term debt that Great Cakes incurred. The business was only required to settle the obligation in 5 years' time; hence the long-term debt was parked under non-current liabilities.

This is extremely important to understand as you'll need this knowledge when we progress to financial ratios in the later chapters of this book. Keep reading.

Cashflow statement

The last financial statement to understand and know, is, the cashflow statement. By learning how to read the cashflow statement (indirect cashflow statement to be exact), we will be able to understand stocks better as we can find out where their cash is flowing, whether is an inflow or an outflow.

Similar to blood in a human body, cash is the blood of a business. Without cash, the business/company will die. Cash is used to purchase inventory, pay out shareholders, settle wages, pay utilities, marketing expenses, the list goes on and on. Cash is what makes the whole economy move. Why was there a financial panic in 2008? Because there was a credit crunch, a lack of cash in the economy. I can't emphasize how important it is to know how to read a cashflow statement.

A company may be reporting profits, but in truth, they can be burning through cash (this is due to accrual based accounting that the income statement recognizes revenue as long as the product is delivered or the service is rendered, a customer may not necessarily have paid in cash for the product yet). So with the cashflow statement, we as investors, can have a sense of where the cash is flowing.

There are 3 main segments in the cashflow statement

1. Cash from operating activities - this segment shows whether a business/company has a net inflow or outflow of cash from their business operations. This segment is very important as shows the true earning power of the business. An example of cash from an operating activity would be, a consumer purchases a piece of cake from a bakery and hands over the cash to the cashier. That is a cash inflow from operating activities. Wages being paid out in cash to workers, that is a cash outflow from operating activities.

2. Cash from investing activities - this segment shows whether a business/company has a net inflow or outflow of cash from their investments. Let me elaborate. An investment can be a purchase in property or equipment, machinery etc. This will reflect as an outflow in cash, from investing activities. If say the company receives dividends from its subsidiaries or joint ventures, this will be a cash inflow from investing activities. Even maintenance work is reflected in investing activities. Hence, more often than not, seasoned investors always want to find out the operating free cash flow of a company/ business (cash after capital expenditures) In other words, cash from operating activities minus cash from

investing activities. If the number is a positive, it means that a company is generating free cash flow.

3. Cash from financing activities - this segment shows the cash inflow or outflow from borrowings from banks or other lenders. For instance, a business/company borrows 10,000 dollars from a bank and gets the money. This is a cash inflow from financing activities. When the company pays down the debt eventually, that will be considered a cash outflow.

In my opinion, understanding the cash flow of a business is the most important statement to understand, for successful stock investing. A word of caution that there were occasions where unethical companies publish fraudulent cash flow statements. You can read about fraudulent cases in the book titled "financial shenanigans". An absolutely excellent read. Now, let's go step by step to see how the Great Cakes' cashflow statement is formed.

Cash from Operating Activities

Cash from Operating Activities	$
Profit for the year	3380
Adjustments:	
Depreciation	1000
Operating cashflows before changes in working capital:	4380

First, we have the cash from operating activities. The profit for the year of $3380 is reflected at the top line. Every cashflow statement will always start with the profit for the year, and this profit number is taken from the profit and loss statement (refer back to the section on the income statement to verify where this number was retrieved).

The cashflow statement for operating activities tend to work backwards, because not all profit reflected in the income statement is converted to cash, so we have to adjust the profit number accordingly to reflect the true amount of cash inflow or outflow.

Remember that depreciation is a non-cash expense but was deducted from profits anyway?

Now, this is where the cash is put back, hence we add $1,000 back to profits. This will bring us to a total of $4,380 in cash generated, before changes in working capital. What the heck is changes in working capital?!

Working capital

This is where things get a little confusing. We know that businesses have current assets and current liabilities, and these are items that are used to run daily operations of businesses and they require cash (buying inventory, buying goods on credit, extending credit to customers etc). These items are also known as working capital, and the sum of all the current assets and liabilities is effectively, working capital. Let's explore how changes in working capital can effectively report cashflow for a business; by comparing Great Cakes' balance sheet at the start and at the end of the fiscal year. (By the way, this confusing method of report cashflow is called the indirect method, and most businesses report cashflow this way, which makes it all the more important to learn this particular method of reporting cashflow).

Beginning

Assets			Liabilities	
Non current assets			**Non current Liabilities**	
Equipment	$5,000		Long term debt	$500
Current assets			**Current Liabilities**	
Cash	$1,000		Short term debt	$500
Inventory	$5,000		Accounts Payable	$0
Accounts receivable	$0			
Total Assets	$11,000		**Total Liabilities**	$1,000
			Owner's Equity	
			Capital	$10,000
			Retained Earnings	$0

Let's take a look at Great Cakes' balance sheet in the beginning. Take note of the underlined accounts and their values. All the underlined accounts (except short term debt) are considered working capital since they belong to the current assets and current liabilities columns. Short term debt is considered a financing activity, that will be reflected in another section of the overall cashflow statement.

End

Assets			Liabilities		
Non current assets			**Non current Liabilities**		
Equipment	$4,000		Long term debt	$500	
Current assets			**Current Liabilities**		
Cash	$7,380		Short term debt	$0	
Inventory	$3,000		Accounts Payable	$1,000	
Accounts receivable	$500				
Total Assets	$14,880		**Total Liabilities**	$1500	

Inventory = 2000 ⬇
Acc. R = 500 ⬆
Acc. P = 1000 ⬆
Short term debt = 500 ⬇

Owner's Equity	
Capital	$10,000
Retained Earnings	$3,380

Before we begin the elaboration, I need you to imagine how the cash flows throughout the different changes in the value of the accounts; whether cash comes in or flows out for every single activity.

Now, let's see the ending values.

First, Inventory has dropped from $5,000 to $3,000, a difference of $2,000. When we look at changes in working capital, we must first ask ourselves, logically, if the value of the business's inventory went down for the year, would the business have bought more inventory? Of course not, since the value of the inventory account went down, it means that the company did not spend money on inventory, in turn showing that cash did not leave the business. So, we must add the shortfall into the cashflow from operating activities.

Second, accounts receivable increased by $500. Did cash come into the business? No, since this is money owed by customers. So, we must subtract the $500 from our cash from operating activities.

Third, accounts payable went up by $1000. Did cash leave the business? No, so we must add back to operating activities as well.

We'll talk about short term debt later.

This is how the cash flow from operating activities will look like after doing all the working capital adjustments.

Cash from Operating Activities	$
Profit for the year	3380
Adjustments:	
Depreciation	1000
Operating cashflows before changes in working capital:	4380
Changes in working capital:	
Accounts Receivable	-500
Inventory	2000
Accounts Payable	1000
Cash generated from Operating Activities	**6880**

And there you have it! The finalised amount of cash generated from operating activities. A grand total of $6,880. Do you see that the net profit for the year does not match the cash generated from operating activities? This is why understanding the cashflow statement is paramount in understanding the true earning power of a business. Let's move on to cash from investing activities.

Cash from Investing Activities

Cash from investing Activities

Equipment	0
Cash generated from investing Activities	**0**

For Great Cakes, it is pretty much straightforward. There was no new equipment purchased, hence no inflow or outflow of cash. If Great Cakes had joint ventures or new equipment or property purchased, the amounts would be reflected here. Basically, any cash regarding investments made by the business will be reflected here.

Cash from Financing Activities

Cash from Financing Activities	$
Short term debt	0
Long term debt	0
Short term debt paid off	-500
Cash generated from Investing Activities	**-500**
Cash at the beginning	1000
Cash at the end	**7380**

Earlier, we saw that short-term debt of $500 was paid off. Hence a negative $500 is reflected in the financing activities section, and no other financing activities were conducted, so the overall cash generated from financing activities was a negative $500.

Add all 3 sections of the cash flow statement together:

Cash from operating activities: $6,880

Cash from investing activities: $0

Cash from financing activities: -$500

This will give us a total value of $6,380. Now, recall Great Cakes' balance sheet at the beginning, the cash account was $1,000. Hence, the cash at the beginning will be reflected as $1,000, and we simply add $6,380 to the beginning cash balance to get our new cash balance of $7,380 (this value is the new cash account value reflected in Great Cakes' ending balance sheet).

The image below shows how a full cashflow statement looks like.

Cash from Operating Activities	$		Cash from Financing Activities	$
Profit for the year	3380		Short term debt	0
			Long term debt	0
Adjustments:			Short term debt paid off	-500
Depreciation	1000			
			Cash generated from Investing Activities	-500
Operating cashflows before changes in working capital:	4380			
			Cash at the beginning	1000
Changes in working capital:				
Accounts Receivable	-500		Cash at the end	7380
Inventory	2000			
Accounts Payable	1000			
Cash generated from Operating Activities	6880			
Cash from investing Activities				
Equipment	0			
Cash generated from investing Activities	0			

By understanding how a cashflow statement is constructed, the investor will have very powerful knowledge on figuring out how much free cash flow a business is generating, which ultimately shows the earning power and value of a business. We'll talk about valuations in the final chapters of this book.

CHAPTER 3

Financial Ratios

Financial ratios are absolutely vital in giving the retail investor critical information about a company's financial health, net worth and earning capabilities. Let's explore some of the main financial ratios.

*Disclaimer: Do not use any of these ratios as a single metric to determine your investment decisions. It is not 100% guaranteed that you will make money just from using these ratios as you can potentially lose all your capital if you do not do additional in-depth research and critical thinking on the prospective company's fundamentals.

Income statement ratios.

Net profit margin

What is the net profit margin? it is a percentage of revenue that is retained as net profits or earnings. To pick the best stocks out there, you as the investor must pick companies with the highest net profit margin (NPM). A company with a high NPM can generate more value for shareholders by earning more profits. In addition, the company has a buffer in the event of an economic downturn. Say earnings dwindle, because the company/business initially had a high NPM, the company will still likely be able to settle all its expenses.

Now let us break down the formula of net profit margin. The values that we need are found the income statement of the company/ business, it is the net profit/ revenue. This will give us the net profit margin.

$$\textbf{Net Profit Margin} = \frac{\textbf{Net Profit}}{\textbf{Revenue}}$$

Using Great Cakes' income statement,

Net profit: $3,380

Revenue: $9,000

The net profit margin is $= \dfrac{\$3,380}{\$9,000}$ = 37.6%

This effectively means that for every 1 dollar of revenue that Great Cakes earns, Great Cakes will get 37.6 cents in profit. Not too shabby.

Net interest cover

What is the net interest cover ratio? To analyse stocks better, the investor must understand how strong a company's/business' earnings are relative to its expenses. There are different types of expenses, operating and non-operating, but one particular expense that can make or break a business, is a debt interest expense. This is expense incurred by borrowing money (taking up loans) from lenders, banks etc. If a business cannot meet its debt expense, or, paying up interest incurred from its loans, the lenders can sue the business, and force the business to sell its assets to return the amount of money owed. And, of course, a business without assets, cannot earn money and this will absolutely demolish shareholder value. Worse still, if a company/business is insolvent (liabilities incurred is more than total value of assets), they won't even be able to settle its debt obligations and would have no choice but to file for bankruptcy and, ultimately, wiping out the shareholders (the value of your stock goes to zero and you lose all your money).

So, how do we find the net interest cover ratio of a company? we use the company's income statement, find the 2 values, net profit, and interest costs (finance costs). Divide net profit by interest costs to get the net interest cover ratio!

$$\text{Net Interest Cover} = \frac{\textbf{Net Profit}}{\textbf{Interest Costs}}$$

Using Great Cakes' income statement,

Net profit: $3,380

Interest Costs: $75

The net interest cover is $= \frac{\$3,380}{\$75}$ = 45 times!

Now let's think for a second, if the net profit is 100 dollars, and the finance costs is 100 dollars, we calculate the net interest cover (100/100) to get a net interest cover ratio of 1. What does this number tell you? Take 3 seconds to think about it, 1 Mississippi, 2 Mississippi, 3 Mississippi.

Is it a good sign that a company can cover its interest costs with their earnings? Of course not! By having a net interest cover of 1, their total interest cost is exactly equal to their earnings, which means they have just enough to cover for obligatory costs so that they do not get sued. This is very risky.

Companies that typically have anything below 4 interest cover ratio is considered risky, so when the investor analyses the business, he would generally be looking for businesses with interest cover ratio of at least 5, there are companies that go as high as 20!

Price to earnings ratio (PE)

What is PE ratio? You hear this term being thrown all around CNBC, Bloomberg, and all other kinds of financial media, but what exactly is it? In a nutshell, it shows how expensive or cheap a company/business/stock is relative to its earnings.

Say you are an investor looking for a business to buy, and a business owner says to you "Hey investor, I would like to sell to you my bakery business at $100,000. Do we have a deal?" What is the first thing that goes through your mind?

As an investor, you need to determine if the business is worth the price that it is selling for in the first place. So how do we determine if a business is worth buying? Every shrewd investor is only looking for one key metric to pique their interest. ROI. Return on Investment. In other words, what is the return on their capital invested in the business. This is where the PE ratio comes into play.

In order to find what the return on capital invested is, we first need to know what the business earnings are for the year. Let's say this bakery earns $10,000 a year. What is its ROI? 10,000/100,000, which gives us 10%. Simple right? Not so fast. As an investor, our other concern is, how long does it take for the investment to earn all its initial capital back? Investors need to know this because the faster we can get our money back, the faster we can compound our holdings by putting the increased returns into other investments, while still maintaining ownership of the initial investment (this is known as free equity). So, investors use the PE ratio to determine the time taken for an investment to make all its capital back; we simply divide the price of business by its earnings for the year.

$$\text{Price to Earnings Ratio (PE ratio)} = \frac{\text{Market Cap of a business (Share Price)}}{\text{Net Profit (Earnings per share)}}$$

Now, back to the example of the bakery business,

we divide 100,000/10,000 and get a value of 10. This number, 10, or a PE ratio of 10, tells us that the business would take 10 years to make all its initial capital back, assuming its earnings remain consistent for future years. PE ratio is an essential in an investor's toolbox to do successful stock picking.

Earnings yield

What is the earnings yield of a business? We hear a lot about the legendary PE ratio, but very rarely encounter the earnings yield.

In order to successfully invest in stocks, the investor must know how much percentage returns he or she is getting out of the capital that was deployed. This is where the earnings yield comes into play.

The idea is simple, take the net profit of the business for year, and divide it by the share price of the business/company. You will then get a percentage that you would have earned from the capital that you took in to buy the stock.

$$\text{Earnings Yield} = \frac{\text{Net Profit (Earnings per share)}}{\text{Market Cap of a business (Share price)}}$$

The mentality of the investor is simple. We are

capital allocators, we find the best place to park money, and watch it grow. So, by using the earnings yield metric to compare the yield on different company earnings, we can decide which is the best option/ which company stock is generating the most yield relative to the capital that we are putting in. Obviously, the higher the yield, the more bang for our buck.

Investors very often use the PE ratio as it measures the number of years an investment takes to gain all its capital back. However, using the earnings yield can portray that same message in another way. Take for instance, a company with a PE ratio of 10, means that an investor will take 10 years to get all his or her money back. Sounds like a long time. Feels expensive? Sure. However, a PE of 10 also means that the investment itself yields 10% per annum, not too shabby now right? It still means the same thing. This is how the earnings yield is presented. Exactly the same as PE technically, but also shows another perspective of the same 2 values in comparison.

The earnings yield is ultimately the inverse of the PE ratio.

Balance sheet ratios

Debt to equity

What is the debt to equity ratio? People often get confused with the debt to equity ratio vs gearing ratio (I will explain this later). There is one major difference, debt to equity compares debt relative to owner's equity (net worth of a company), whereas gearing compares debt relative to total assets.

To practice conservative investing, of course the investor needs to know and rely on both essential ratios. Let's first define what is debt and equity separately.

Debt - money that a company has borrowed and is required to pay back, with interest, at a later date. Now, if the company fails to meet the payment deadlines, the lenders can potentially sue the business and force it to sell its assets to pay the money back. If a business has to sell its assets, especially if it's at a bad time, they can incur a loss on those assets as well, leading to massive loss in shareholder value. The stock price itself will most definitely be hammered and can very likely lead to the company going into bankruptcy protection (I don't have to tell what happens to the value of your stock holdings if the company that you bought reaches to this stage).

Equity - the net worth of a company. Imagine this. A company decides to cease business operations and stop running the business altogether, the owner will first sell of all its assets and get a sum of money for it. Next, the owner will pay off all existing liabilities that the business has incurred, using those proceeds. The remaining sum of money is the equity. In other words, it is the net share holder interest, shareholder's equity, or owner's equity (they all mean the same thing).

Now that we have defined debt and equity, we simply take those 2 values (found in the balance sheet) and divide the debt by equity. This percentage will give the amount of debt relative to the company's total net worth. Now why is this important? The lower this percentage, the more confidence the investors will have in knowing that the company has the resources to settle its debt obligations (and not requiring bankruptcy protection). This is one crucial ratio that every investor must use when doing their initial due diligence on a prospective stock.

$$\text{Debt to Equity ratio} = \frac{\textbf{Total Debt}}{\textbf{Total Equity}}$$

Using Great Cakes' balance sheet,

Total debt: $500 (long term debt)

Total equity: $13,380 (capital plus retained earnings)

The debt to equity ratio is $= \frac{\$500}{\$13,380} = 3.7\%$

Great Cakes is super conservative in their borrowings. You can't go bankrupt if you have no debt.

Return on Equity

Another metric with regards to shareholder equity is the return on equity (ROE) ratio. This metric is crucial in understanding the capital allocation effectiveness of a business. Remember, every business owner, investor or CEO, must learn how to allocate capital properly. For example, if a CEO decides to spend $100 million dollars on research and development, he or she must anticipate how much returns he or she can get through that investment in research and development. In other words, the higher the return on equity, the more effective the business is at producing returns.

Return on Equity=(Net Profit)/(Total Equity)

Using Great Cakes' balance sheet and income statement,

Total equity: $13,380 (capital plus retained earnings)

Net profit: $3,380

The return on equity is =$3,380/$13,380 = 25.3%

Current ratio

What is current ratio? It is a fundamental financial ratio to indicate how liquid a company is in the short term. The higher the number, the more conservative the business/ company. By knowing this simple ratio, you can invest in stocks conservatively.

Let me elaborate. The current ratio can be found by using 2 values in the balance sheet, the current assets and the current liabilities. As you know, the word current means, that the asset can be readily liquidated for cash, and liabilities that need to be settled within a year. If say a business has no choice but to settle a number of liabilities by the end of the year, we as investors need to ensure that they have sufficient cash readily available to settle these liabilities. Of course, a business can't possibly hold everything in cash, it will be rotting away and losing value through inflation. They have, however, assets that are liquid enough to be sold quickly, like inventory or accounts receivable. So, if the total current asset value exceeds the total current liabilities, or at least have equal value, we know that by and large the company is able to tide through the years' worth of liabilities.

$$\text{Current Ratio} = \frac{\text{Current Assets}}{\text{Current Liabilities}}$$

Using Great Cakes' balance sheet,

Current assets: $10,880

Current liabilities: $1,000

The current ratio is $= \frac{\$10,880}{\$1,000} = 10.9$

Great Cakes, as mentioned earlier, is grossly conservative. They have 10 times as much current assets as liabilities. A rock-solid balance sheet.

Quick ratio

The quick ratio is similar to the current ratio. It reflects the liquidity of the company in the short term, minus its inventory holdings. By doing this, the investor is being even cautious, and will tend to pick stocks more conservatively.

The formula is the same as the current ratio, with one added part, inventory is omitted from current assets. So, the formula will look like this, (current assets - inventory)/ current liabilities. Now, why do we as investors need this additional step? Because sometimes, inventory can expire; certain perishable goods with a short shelf life like basic food supplies, bread, meats, can rot and lose value very quickly. Hence, we cannot take into consideration the value of inventory since it tends to deteriorate very quickly if it is not sold. This is contrary to say a steel production company, whereby its finished goods have a longer shelf life and its value does not diminish too quickly.

$$\text{Quick Ratio} = \frac{\text{Current Assets} - \text{Inventory}}{\text{Current Liabilities}}$$

Using Great Cakes' balance sheet,

Current assets: $10,880

Inventory: $3,000

Current liabilities: $1,000

The quick ratio is $= \frac{\$10,880 - \$3,000}{\$1,000}$ = 7.9

The quick ratio is often used for consumer staples likes super marts, and other F&B companies and commodities companies (pork carcass, bread, oil palm).

Gearing ratio

The gearing ratio is an absolutely essential ratio to know. This powerful ratio can not only help the investor to invest in stocks safely, but it can also act as metric to see if a company has any room for expansion. The formula for gearing ratio is simply total debt divided by total assets. It measures the amount of debt the company has relative to its assets. The lower the number, the more stable a company/business is. Why? Because they have assets to cover for the debt in case the earnings or investments made by the company goes sour.

$$\text{Gearing ratio} = \frac{\textbf{Total Debt}}{\textbf{Total Assets}}$$

Using Great Cakes' balance sheet,

Total debt: $500

Total assets: $14,880

The gearing ratio is $= \dfrac{\$500}{\$14,880} = 3.4\%$

Typically, a company with a 30~% gearing is considered stable, however do not assume that it is completely risk free. Nothing is risk free in this world. In the end, even though the gearing is low, if the company can't sell off the assets it has in its books to settle the debt obligations (times of downturn there will be less buyers who want to buy assets, or at least, the assets can be sold at bargain basement prices), they would still need to declare bankrupt. However, always take investing as a probability game because the investor is bound to make mistakes. As an investor, you want to make sure that your mistakes are not too costly that it wipes out all your capital.

Sorry for the sermon, back to gearing ratio. So, companies who use this metric often in their financial reports are REITs, because their business model typically relies on debt (they borrow money to buy real estate and collect rental income). Now, if a REIT's gearing is low, not only are they more conservative and stable, but they also have room to expand. A REIT, and the governing body that regulates it, will always have a mandate to say that a REIT cannot go past, say, 40% in gearing, so, if a REIT has only 30% gearing at that point in time, they can effectively borrow 10% more money (debt headroom) and buy more real estate, in turn augmenting rental income and profits to shareholders accordingly.

Book value

What is book value? the book value of a company represents the net worth of a company. Imagine a situation where a company decides to stop business, for whatever reason. What is the process for ending a business? The owner will first sell off all the business' assets, use the proceeds to pay off all existing liabilities, and the remaining amount is the book value. In other words, it is the owner's equity/ Shareholder's interest/ shareholder's equity.

Book value of a business
= Total Assets – Total Liabilities.

Why is this metric an important part of stock valuation? Say a company is selling in the stock market at 15 dollars a share, and we also know that the book value of that same company is at 20 dollars a share, wouldn't this mean that the market is pricing that same business 5 dollars less than what it is actually worth? Yes! This is the main reason why we need to know how to calculate the book value of a company; to have a reasonable stock valuation benchmark. The book value of a company will give the investor an idea of whether a stock is selling cheap or expensive, relative to what it is worth.

Price to book value (PBV)

This metric was first used by the father of value investing, Mr Benjamin Graham. He was very quantitative in his investment approach; He used the net shareholder's interest/owner's equity/ shareholder's equity as his benchmark for his stock purchase. His iconic stock valuation method went on to inspire the greatest investor of all time, Warren Buffet, to study under Mr. Graham, and Buffet applied the PBV method at the start of his investing career. He went on to make tons of money practicing this method.

Price to Book Value Ratio

$$= \frac{\textbf{Market Cap of a business}}{\textbf{Total Equity}}$$

Using Great Cakes' balance sheet, and assuming that Great Cakes is selling at $20,000 in the stock market,

Market Cap of Great Cakes: $20,000

Total equity: $13,380

The price to book value ratio is $= \frac{\$20,000}{\$13,380} = 1.49$

This number effectively means that Great Cakes is currently selling at almost 50% more than what it is worth in its balance sheet.

There are a number of arguments and thoughts regarding this archaic method of investing. Some people say that it is outdated, and not really usable in this day and age. Some are still hardcore practitioners, check out Seth Klarman and the late Walter Schloss.

The truth is, there are seasons for every method of investing. In darker times, like the great depression era, stocks were frowned up and trashed, leaving their prices to be a lot less than what they were actually worth. Companies were selling at PBV of as little as 0.2! (the company was selling at a massive bargain as it was selling at 20% of what its assets were worth in its books). In this day and age, people look more towards growth and future earnings, hence leading to less of such opportunities in the investment market. Investors are now willing to pay more for stocks, way more than what a stock is worth on paper. In addition, because more and more people know and practice this method of investing over the years, the good PBV opportunities tend to get snapped up quickly by investors, since there are more of such players in the market now.

Beware the sayings of another legendary Investor, Sir John Templeton. His famous quote is "Bull markets are born on pessimism, grow on scepticism, mature on optimism and die on euphoria." There will be a point, in every market cycle, when the last buyer of equities realize, "wait a minute, this stock is way too expensive, I'd better not buy it", and so starts the collapse of the stock market. And, as every bear market comes to its end, bargain opportunities will start to reappear again, and, if it does, be ready for it, for the knowledge of PBV will aid you in your quest to capitalize on bargain stocks, and ultimately meeting your financial destiny.

Margin of safety

What is margin of safety? Imagine an engineer being tasked to build a bridge above a river, meant for a single 5-ton vehicle to cross over. Would the engineer design the bridge just to be able to support 5 tons? Of course not! There is just too much at stake! the lives of the drivers and workers, the valuable raw material that the vehicle is transporting etc. Should the bridge collapse, it will a horrible nightmare for those involved in the journey. Hence, the engineer will build the bridge in such a way that it can support than 5 tonnes, because he knows that there is chance that his estimations could be wrong.

There will always be "what ifs" to consider for this this sort of planning, as we know that murphy's law is prevalent everywhere (anything that can go wrong will go wrong). Investing is no exception. As the engineer designs his structure with the ultimate goal of protecting the people, raw materials and the vehicles that use the bridge, so too does the investor protect his capital in the event of an incorrect judgement.

Let's elaborate using a stock valuation model.

Scenario 1: Say the net worth of a business is $50,000 and the market is quoting you a price of $60,000. Is there a margin of safety embedded in the price? No, it does not, because the price is $10,000 higher than the what the business is actually worth.

Scenario 2: the market is quoting $50,000, is there a margin of safety? NO, because we are buying the business for exactly what it is worth on its books. Let me tell you it is not wisest choice to buy at exactly what a business is worth. Remember how I always say that you have to take the numbers in the financial statements with a pinch of salt? Well, sometimes, balance sheets may quote a certain net book value, but in truth, the assets can't be sold for the value that was quoted on the balance sheet itself, for a whole host of reasons (obsolete, outdated, spoilt etc.). This is why we need to have a margin of safety when we make a buy decision, to ensure that we limit our losses in case we are wrong in our valuation.

Scenario 3: the market is quoting you $25,000 for the business. Good deal? YES! margin of safety embedded in the price? YES, because the market is now quoting you a price that is 50% of what the business is worth on its books. This gives you a buffer to not lose so much money in the event that you are wrong in your analysis. Even if the business was able to liquidate itself only at 75% of its net book value, which adds up to $37,500, you as the investor will still make a whopping 50% ON YOUR CAPITAL! Since you bought the business at $25,000 and got back $37,500. This is why margin of safety is so important. IF you had bought the business at exactly what it was worth, and the owners could only liquidate the business for 75%. you would have lost 25% of your capital instead.

The margin of safety concept is indeed, one of the most, if not the most important principle if you want to invest conservatively.

CHAPTER 4

Dividends

"**D**o you know the only thing that gives me pleasure? It's to see my dividends coming in." - John D Rockefeller
What is a dividend? 2 words. Passive income. For all you capitalist pigs reading this, a dividend is cold hard cash paid out to company shareholders periodically, as a show of good faith to reward them for putting their hard-earned capital into these companies. In addition, companies with a long dividend track record usually have an easier time attracting investors for funding, as a strong dividend record is a show of a company's solid earnings.

These companies are usually older, matured companies who can't deploy the cash that they have earned into other business ventures or investments that can yield good returns, so they just simply pay a sum of these earnings back to the shareholders. Companies like this have sort of a premier status in the stock market world, "dividend aristocrats" as investors would call them.

For retail investors like us, we can invest in solid dividend paying companies to provide us with a steady stream of cash flow, for as long as the company can pay it. That is why we need to understand dividends, and why we always MUST have a portion of our investment portfolio as dividend paying companies. The income that dividend paying companies provide will support you in future. IF you are focused enough, You can even accumulate so much of dividend paying companies that when the income they provide finally exceeds your expenses, you can breathe a sigh of relief because, even though you lose your job, or your ability to earn, you still have a steady income stream that can settle your utilities, food, mortgage etc., without you having to work for it.

Companies that tend to pay good, steady dividends usually provide essentials for daily living, or items that are used very regularly, for example, soap and shampoo (Johnson and Johnson's), post-it(3M), healthcare (Abbot), telecom

(AT&T), petrol (Chevron), drinks (Coke), toothpaste (Colgate), peanut butter (Hormel Foods), tissue paper and diapers (Kimberly- Clark), food (McDonald's), cleaning agents (Procter and Gamble), hyper marts (Walmart); these companies have track records of paying dividends consistently, even through every recession and bear market, for as long as 30-40 years! Some even 60 years! These businesses are seen as very reliable for providing cash to shareholders, even during darker financial times.

As a result of their reliable earnings and consistent payouts, they are classified as defensive stocks. Defensive stocks are less volatile in nature (their stock price doesn't fluctuate as much as other companies), but personally i find them both defensive and offensive, the best of both worlds. Dividend companies, especially those that grow their dividends, have often beaten stock market indices. (just look up Hersh Cohen, a great fund manager who is a proponent for dividend investing). Forget all the hype about hi-tech growth companies.Go for the old, boring, cash spitting companies that generate CASH like there's no tomorrow. What better deal can you ask for than for your investments to return capital back to you? In about 10-20 years' time, you can recoup ALL your principal back, and still own the company! And it will be obediently paying you cold hard cash, day in day out, every single year. Even as you sleep like the capitalist pig that you are.

Dividend yield

What is dividend yield? It is the amount of cash that an investment can generate relative to the purchase price of the business, expressed as a percentage. Income investors, or dividend investors, use this key metric very often to make investment decisions on whether or not a stock is worth buying.

So how do we calculate the dividend yield? We need to take the declared dividend amount by the company and divide that amount by the price that the investor had bought the business at. The higher the dividend yield, the harder our capital is working for us.

Typically, with current market stock prices, you can easily find average companies nowadays generating around 3~5% dividend yield; premium companies will usually have a lower yield, 1~2%, because they are more expensive. Always remember that the yield is dependent on the current price of the business that the market is selling at. So, as an investor, how do we increase this yield? Of course, we need to wait for an opportunity where stock prices are lower.

Shrewd dividend investors tend to lie and wait in the weeds, patiently hoping to capitalize on a bear market season to snap up great companies at low prices. If you had spare cash during say, the 2008 recession, you would have been able buy a supremely defensive and strong company like Johnson and Johnson at $50 a share, with a dividend of $1.62. That gives us a dividend yield of 3.5%. This dividend yield, for a sterling company like Johnson and Johnson, is only available probably once in 10~15 years. Now fast forward to 2020, guess what their dividend is now. $3.75. Their dividends grew by 131%! Insane. Totally insane. Assuming you held on to J & J, you would be yielding a whopping 7.5% from a blue-chip company, that has close to no chance in losing market share or going bankrupt for that matter, not forgetting all those years of earning at least 3.5% dividend yield. You think this is it? There's more! Not only did dividends increase, check out what happened to their stock price. As of today, 31/5/2020, their current stock price is selling at $148. 196% increase. Let's do a calculation on what your ROI is.

Dividend yield from 2009 to 2020 (conservatively) = 11 years X 3.5 = 38.5%

Capital appreciation = 196%

Total ROI = 196 + 38.5 = 234.5%

Who says the retail investor can't get rich? if you had the iron in your veins to invest a sum of say $100,000 in solid recession proof dividend paying stocks during 2008, you would be sitting on a pot of at least $234,000 today. My calculations above are ultra conservative because I did not take into account the dividend growth. Too much work. Anyway, I'll leave you with a saying," Never let a good crisis go to waste." - Winston Churchill

Of course there are arguments that we can just do passive investing and be done with it, but the thing about passive investing is that even though benchmark indices like S and P have 500 companies in them, the overall market capitalization is dominated by just a few companies; If I'm not mistaken, FACEBOOK, APPLE, AMAZON-,NETFLIX, GOOGLE (FAANG) make up 15% of the whole S and P 500 index. 500 companies in the index, and 15% dominated by 4 companies. It is really skewed. In addition, the FAANG stocks don't pay out dividends as they can grow it better if it is reinvested.

So, let me ask you, when you hit your capital appreciation targets and liquidate your S and P position, what are you going to do with that money? You can let it sit in your bank and you slowly chip away at it until the day you meet your maker. Yes, the lump sum should be substantial, but let's say you outlive your savings and proceeds. What then? Think about it. It is wiser to build a portfolio that can constantly generate income, and accumulate to a point where the dividend yield of your overall portfolio can cover your yearly expenses, you'd have a better sense of assurance that you'll have income, till you meet your maker.

Dividend pay-out ratio

Now that we have discussed about dividends, and dividend yield, we need to understand another crucial metric: the dividend payout ratio. What is the dividend payout ratio? This ratio measures the amount of dividends paid out to shareholders from its net profit. In other words, it tells us the likelihood of companies being able to sustain their dividends through their yearly earnings. Let me illustrate with 2 examples.

Say a cake company (Great Cakes) earns $10,000 in net profit for 2020. They then declared an $8,000 dividend payout. As an investor, what are the questions going through your head now? Firstly, of course, it is good that we are receiving a nice cash payout. However, the deeper question for income investors to answer is, why did we buy the stock in the first place? Is it for capital appreciation? Or for a recurring yield every single year. As per my previous chapter on dividends, income/dividend investors tend to buy companies that can provide regular, recurring, and sustainable cash payouts. So, relating back to Great Cakes, we can see that they earned $10,000 for the year, and are paying out $8,000, which effectively means that they are able to afford to pay out their dividends, since their earnings exceed their dividends.

Now let's have another scenario. The same company Great Cakes earns $10,000 in profits but declares an $11,000 dividend payout instead. On the one hand, it's a hefty sum of money and investors will most definitely be satisfied. However, as an income investor, what can we say about the sustainability of Great Cake's dividends? Do you think that they really can continue to pay $11,000 regularly? Of course not, as their dividends exceed their annual profits. This is why the dividend payout ratio is an extremely meaningful metric for investors.

Why would companies want to pay out more than they can afford? It is a sticky situation for companies. This is where dividend yields come in. Firstly, we have to understand that management compensation schemes are by and large linked to the stock price of the company. So, if say, Great Cakes' stock price were to increase to the management's KPI, management bonuses will be good. Now, dividend paying companies are usually priced by the market according to their ability to maintain their dividends, and their dividend yields. So imagine if Great Cakes was known to pay out sustainable dividends of $11,000 for the past 10 years, and over time, earnings dwindle, the Great Cakes management would still want to, as best as they can, maintain their stock price of Great Cakes (so that they can continue to earn their bonuses). Hence, they make a decision to maintain their dividend payments even though their annual net profits cannot sustain it. Another reason would be, that some companies, like bank stocks, rely a lot on outside capital; having a solid and sustainable dividend paying history would make it easier for the banks to attract investors and precious capital, so even though their earnings can't afford it, they might still agree to a high dividend amount that exceeds net profits, to show investors of their commitment to pay out steady dividends, and also to display confidence that earnings will improve in the following year and that they are more than willing to pay out high amounts in dividends.

Different industries and different types of companies have different levels of acceptable payout ratios. For example, REITs are mandated to have at least 90% dividend payout ratio. Other companies, like utilities, radio stations and telecom companies, also have reasonably high payout ratios (between 70~90%) because they have little opportunities for expansion and/or require little capital expenditure. Remember that from our previous chapter, companies pay out dividends because they have grown to maturity and have difficulty expanding and using their cash as effectively as before, so they pass a portion of this cash to the shareholders instead. Companies that are in the growing stages of their business cycle tend to have a low payout ratio, or even a zero percent payout ratio (because they require the cash to expand, and of course they can grow that cash more effectively than their shareholders can). A good attribute of a low payout ratio also means that the company has the potential to increase dividends, and if that particular company is committed to increasing dividends, your net worth will grow exponentially, and in double time as well.

CHAPTER 5

Finance Concepts

"A dollar today is worth more than a dollar tomorrow." What do you understand by this statement? Let's discuss the concept of the time value of money. Money, in its nominal terms, does not reflect its true value, as there is always a time factor involved before you can find what money is truly worth.

Let us use a scenario to illustrate the time value of money. Imagine it is the year 2015, and $60 can buy you 3 cakes. Fast forward to 2020, now, the same $60 can only buy you 2 cakes. In nominal terms, it is the same amount of money, $60, however, it has lost its original buying power of 3 cakes 5 years before, as that same $60 can buy less goods than 5 years ago. Hence, the same $60 in 2015 is worth more than $60 in 2020.

Why does this phenomenon happen? Inflation. As population grows, productivity and wealth increases, leading to more demand for goods and services. This will inevitably cause the general price of goods to rise, hence, a dollar today will not be able to buy the same amount of goods as compared to the past.

This rudimentary concept of money is crucial in finance and investing as well. Next, I will explain about the present value of money.

Present value of money

Now we know that the real value of money decreases with time, can we put a numerical value on money in the future? Yes, we can, but it will never be an accurate representation of what it is truly worth. At best, it can only be an estimation. This is where the present value of money comes into play. Let us use an example to illustrate this concept.

Assume that we as investors are presented with an investment opportunity: Great Cakes, a cake company, is projected to earn $1,000 per year from this year, 2020, and 4 years after that. So, we have 5 years' worth of earnings, $1,000 per year, giving us a total of $5,000 of profits in 5 years. Now, is the sum of profits worth $5,000 today (in 2020)? Of course not! Why? Because inflation will occur and deteriorate the yearly earnings' real value over time. Hence, we need to discount each year's real value to find the present value of the sum of earnings over 5 years. This is how we estimate the present value of money. In relation to investing, if we were to value the business, we would not buy the business at $5,000 because we know that the value of its future earnings relative to today's (present) value will be a lot less than $5,000.

So now, let us find the present value of the sum of its earnings. Firstly, we know that on average, inflation causes price levels to increase by about 1~2% compounded every year, which effectively means, the value of money will deteriorate by that same amount every year. Secondly, each year's earnings are a year later than the previous year, so, the real value of each year's earnings is less than the previous year's earnings, hence, it is must be discounted more with each passing year. We require the use present value table to find the amount we need to discount with each year (google "Present value table" for the whole range of interest rates, for now I'll just crop the table for easier reading).

Assuming a 3% erosion of value from inflation...compounded.

Present Value Table

Periods (n)	1%	2%	3%	4%	5%	6%
1	0.990	0.980	0.971	0.962	0.952	0.943
2	0.980	0.961	0.943	0.925	0.907	0.890
3	0.971	0.942	0.915	0.889	0.864	0.840
4	0.961	0.924	0.888	0.855	0.823	0.792
5	0.951	0.906	0.863	0.822	0.784	0.747
6	0.942	0.888	0.837	0.790	0.746	0705
7	0.933	0.871	0.813	0.760	0.711	0.665
8	0.923	0.853	0.789	0.731	0.677	0.627
9	0.914	0.837	0.766	0.703	0.645	0.592
10	0.905	0.820	0.744	0.676	0.614	0.558
11	0.896	0.804	0.722	0.650	0.585	0.527
12	0.887	0.788	0.701	0.625	0.557	0.497
13	0.879	0.773	0.681	0.601	0.530	0.469
14	0.870	0.758	0.661	0.577	0.505	0.442
15	0.861	0.743	0.642	0.555	0.481	0.417
16	0.853	0.728	0.623	0.534	0.458	0.394
17	0.844	0.714	0.605	0.513	0.436	0.371
18	0.836	0.700	0.587	0.494	0.416	0.350
19	0.828	0.686	0.570	0.475	0.396	0.331
20	0.820	0.673	0.554	0.456	0.377	0.312

Interest rates (r)

Let's use a conservative inflation growth rate of 3%. So, we select the 3% interest rate column, and we take the value of the first 4 rows (periods) in the 3% column. If you look at the values (highlighted in the red box), Period 1 has a value of 0.971. This means that for year 1, the $1,000 must be discounted to 0.971 of its numerical value. This will leave us with a real value of 0.971 x $1,000 = $971. This is the present value of earnings in year 1 (2021), relative to today, year 0 (2020). If we move on to calculate the real value of each year, it would be as follows:

Year 2 (2022) – 0.943 X $1,000 = $943

Year 3 (2023) – 0.915 X $1,000 = $915

Year 4 (2024) – 0.888 X $1,000 = $888

Not forgetting the current Year 0 (2020), earning $1,000, we have a total present value of:

$1,000 (year 0) + $971 (year 1) + $943 (year 2) + $915 (year 3) + $888 (year 4) = $4,717.

From this, we know that the $5,000 sum of profits is actually worth about $4,717 in present value. Hence, from an investor's standpoint, it is not logical to base the fair value of the business just from the numerical/ nominal value of its anticipated earnings; the investor must discount its yearly earnings by some percentage rate in order to get the present monetary value of the business itself.

Discount rate

Now that we understand how to calculate the present value of money, we must question ourselves on what an appropriate rate is to use to discount earnings. Keeping in mind that the discount rate is completely subjective, it is a percentage that an investor deems acceptable to deduct future earnings/ cashflow, to bring these forecasted earnings/ cashflow back to present value. In other words, the inflation rate used previously is an example of a discount rate! The discount rate is a concept rather than an absolute number, and this discount rate varies with each investor. Let us use 2 examples to illustrate this point.

Using the previous example on explaining the present value of money, if an investor were to use a discount rate of 3%, the business would be valued at $4,717. However, if the investor changes his discount rate to 8%, the valuation will be as follows:

Assuming an 8% erosion of value ...compounded.

Present Value Table

	Interest rates (r)					
4%	5%	6%	7%	8%	9%	10%
0.962	0.952	0.943	0.935	0.926	0.917	0.909
0.925	0.907	0.890	0.873	0.857	0.842	0.826
0.889	0.864	0.840	0.816	0.794	0.772	0.751
0.855	0.823	0.792	0.763	0.735	0.708	0.683
0.822	0.784	0.747	0.713	0.681	0.650	0.621
0.790	0.746	0705	0.666	0.630	0.596	0.564
0.760	0.711	0.665	0.623	0.583	0.547	0.513
0.731	0.677	0.627	0.582	0.540	0.502	0.467
0.703	0.645	0.592	0.544	0.500	0.460	0.424
0.676	0.614	0.558	0.508	0.463	0.422	0.386
0.650	0.585	0.527	0.475	0.429	0.388	0.350
0.625	0.557	0.497	0.444	0.397	0.356	0.319
0.601	0.530	0.469	0.415	0.368	0.326	0.290
0.577	0.505	0.442	0.388	0.340	0.299	0.263
0.555	0.481	0.417	0.362	0.315	0.275	0.239
0.534	0.458	0.394	0.339	0.292	0.252	0.218
0.513	0.436	0.371	0.317	0.270	0.231	0.198
0.494	0.416	0.350	0.296	0.250	0.212	0.180
0.475	0.396	0.331	0.277	0.232	0.194	0.164
0.456	0.377	0.312	0.258	0.215	0.178	0.149

Year 0 (2020) - $1,000

Year 1 (2021) – 0.926 X $1,000 = $926

Year 2 (2022) – 0.857 X $1,000 = $857

Year 3 (2023) – 0.794 X $1,000 = $794

Year 4 (2024) – 0.735 X $1,000 = $735

The total present value of the business would be $1,000 +$926 +$857 +$794 + $735 = $4,312

We can see that the first scenario shows a higher

present value ($4,717) compared to the second scenario ($4,312). If the business was selling at $4,500, the first discount rate of 3% would have warranted a purchase, whereas the second discount rate of 8% would have not. What does this tell you? The higher the discount rate, the less likely an investor will want to make a purchase (since the present value would most likely be lower than the quoted price).

Ultimately, it is entirely up to the investor on which discount rate he or she uses, with different consequences for each path (when I say "path", I mean comparing an investor who uses a higher vs a lower discount rate.) If an investor is more aggressive, he or she will use a lower discount rate, as it would give the investor more leeway in his or her valuations; if markets go up, the investor will get exposed to more upside because the investor will tend to be more liberal in valuations , leading to more liberal buying decisions, It goes the same for downside, investors who are aggressive in discount rates potentially expose themselves to losing more capital compared to a more conservative investor who uses a higher discount rate.

The conservative investor, on the other hand, uses a high discount rate, and this would increase the likelihood of him or her having less probability (but not zero) of making a capital-losing purchase, as a high discount rate would usually represent an extremely discounted valuation. This would lead to more strict rules for purchasing stocks and likely to only make prudent purchases during down markets (if the conservative investor is indeed disciplined and bold enough).

You might think, since that is the case, why not just use a high discount rate? Now, statistically, markets go up 60~% of the time. So technically, if you are making less purchases, you will tend to miss more upside potential in your own portfolio. With this dilemma, what is a proper discount rate to use? The answer will be in my chapter: The risk-free rate.

Risk-free rate

Let us study the term, RISK FREE, meaning free of risk, riskless, without any danger or probability of losing capital. What is the only asset class that you can think of that is riskless? If you do not know, it is government issued debt, or government bonds. Treasury bills, notes etc. Why is it risk free? Because the government guarantees to pay the interest and the principal back to the investor once the bond matures. Hence the term, risk free. So, if government bonds can guarantee the investor say, a 4% annual interest, plus a return of the full principal at maturity, why would any investor put their money in a riskier asset class like equities if equities yield the same 4% return? The investor yields the same return as a government bond, but stands a chance to lose all his capital, it would not be rational for the investor to put his money into equities.

With this rationale in mind, investors often use the risk free rate as the discount rate to value their stock purchases; it is the minimum return that their investment must make in order for the investment to be worthwhile (since the risk free rate guarantees their capital on top of the promised interest rate payment). In other words, the risk-free rate can be described as the cost of capital, since by not putting our capital inside a risk-free asset, we are technically losing money.

The risk-free rate is never standard, I could go deeper into how governments determine the coupon payments of their bonds (monetary policy etc), but I'm no economist, so I will not attempt to explain it. As investors, let's keep things simple. All we need to do is, watch what the current risk-free rate of the treasury bills are, and amend our valuations as the risk-free rate changes.

Hurdle rate

Now that we understand the discount rate and risk-free rate, let's talk about the hurdle rate. Honestly, the concept is the same. However, instead of using inflation rates, or treasury bond yields, Investors can use the overall stock market returns as the hurdle rate. Why?

If you think about it, ultimately, this is the rate that every investor should at least match, the overall market return, or a benchmark index, like the S & P 500, or Dow Jones Industrial Average, as it is the most fuss free and simple strategy, index investing. 96% of all mutual fund managers never beat the benchmark index returns over a prolonged period (10 – 20 years), and if you can utilise the hurdle rate to discount your forecasts, and be right in your investment decisions, you will be among the 4% of financial unicorns that actually beat the market returns.

In conclusion, I decided to explain the various types of rates that investors use for valuation, because as a budding investor, I was confused by all these terms. I would like to share with you that the inflation rate, hurdle rate, risk-free rate, is all the same! It basically means to discount your forecasts to a rate that you are most comfortable with. Forget about WACC, CAPM, IRR and all the other mumbo jumbo that you read in financial textbooks, leave those formulas to the fancy quants and hedge fund managers.

As a retail investor who picks individual stocks, think simple, think like a businessman, envision where the profits and cash flow to, and this mindset will give you the greatest probability in making sound investment decisions. Even then, you may not be able to beat the market. So, an easier option would be, just buy the whole flippin' market and index your savings! Let your wealth grow with the biggest companies that serve the economy, and you will beat 96% of all the fund managers over the long run. Go look up Jack Bogle and passive investing. It's a game changer, the passive investing strategy is almost a sure win, albeit very boring. A boring way to get rich. Just to quote Mr Bogle, " Put aside a sum of money in an index fund at 25, don't look at it, don't peek, check it again when you're 65, be sure a doctor is nearby to resuscitate you, because you will be shocked by the amount of money that has compounded for you, just by putting it in an index fund."

Compounded annual growth rate (CAGR)

Compounded annual growth rate. Investors use this metric to gauge how much a company grows on average every year, so that forecasts can be made on future growth. Let's say Great Cakes grows from $13,000 in net earnings to $15,000 in 5 years, how do we find out how much they grew annually on a compounded basis? By using this formula:

[(Ending value/ Beginning value) ^ (1/ No. of years)] - 1

Step 1: Divide the ending value ($15,000) by the beginning value ($13,000). You should get a value of 1.153.

Step 2: Exponentially multiply 1.153 by the inverse of the number of periods the company took to grow from $13,000 to $15,000. Take note that although the duration is 5 years, we use 4 periods because, well, there are 4 periods in between the 5 years (look at the image below to understand what I'm saying here). So, the inverse of 4 is ¼, or 0.25. 1.153^0.25 will give a value of 1.036.

Step 3: Subtract 1 from that value (1.036) to get a CAGR of 0.036, or 3.6%!

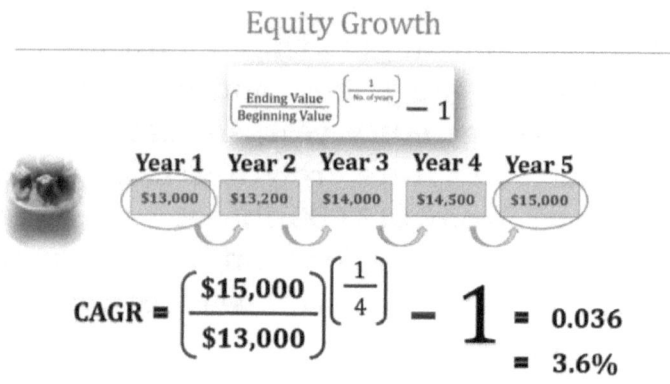

Equity Growth

The final percentage tells us that Great Cakes grew at a compounded rate of 3.6% for the past years, which also means that chances are, based on past historical performance, that Great Cakes can continue to grow at a rate of 3.6% for the foreseeable future.

Of course, there are certain limitations. In no way should the CAGR be used as a guaranteed growth rate, as business fundamentals can deteriorate, ultimately leading a slowdown in growth. Secondly, we only used 5 years' worth of historical data. Company performance does not always move upwards in a straight line, there are good years and bad years, so a better gauge would be to use a longer historical time range to smoothen out any irregularities. 10 years of past financial performance would be recommended when calculating CAGR.

CHAPTER 6

Intrinsic Value

You have made it to last segment of this book, learning to calculate the intrinsic value, congratulations on making it through thus far. Let's get down to the nitty gritty.

Firstly, what is intrinsic value? The intrinsic value is the assumed true value of a stock, considering the amount of cash that it can generate over time. This is different from the price to book value model that we discussed earlier. This intrinsic value model calculates the total value of all the cash that a business can generate over its life, whereas the book value model calculates what the company is worth; it does not take into consideration its earning power, but rather, the assets in its books. Both valuation models are important. The intrinsic value calculation that is explained here is very similar to the discounted cash flow model (google it if you would like to find out).

The Oracle of Omaha himself, Mr Warren Buffet, describes the intrinsic value clearly, " What is the number, that if you were all-knowing about the future, and you can predict all the cash that the business can give you between now and judgement day, discounted at the proper discount rate, that number is what the intrinsic value of a business is. In other words, the only reason for making an investment, laying out money now, is to get more money later on, that's what investing is all about."

The intrinsic value calculation is broken down into 6 steps.

Step 1: Look back to the past 10 years of the company's financial performance and find its CAGR. Find out its free cash flow growth for the past 10 years.

Finding the free cash flow is not easy, there are 2 ways to do this, the more manual way is to go to a company's cashflow statement and do a rough estimation from there. Subtract cash from investing activities from cash from operating activities. This would more or less give you the free cash flow of a business. Alternatively, you can search for "free cash flow" in the annual report and see if anything pops up. Companies occasionally state what their free cash flow is. You may choose to use earnings as well, but as mentioned previously, earnings can sometimes be manipulated, so the most straightforward way is to see the cash. It is the most meaningful representation of a business's earning power.

Once you have collected the data, commence your CAGR calculation. Let's imagine that Great Cakes generated free cash flow of $3,000 in 2010, and $11,000 in 2020, this gives us a CAGR of 13.8%, not too shabby.

$$CAGR = [(\$11,000/\$3,000) \wedge (1/10)] - 1 = 13.8\%$$

Case Study

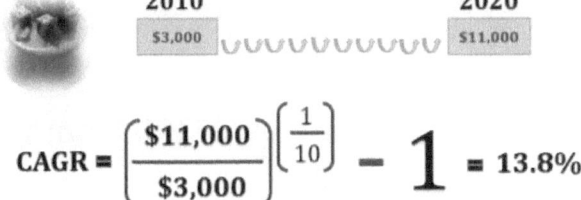

Step 1: Look back to the past 10 years of the company's financial performance and find its CAGR. Find out its free cash flow growth for the past 10 years.

2010   2020

$3,000 $11,000

$$\text{CAGR} = \left(\frac{\$11,000}{\$3,000} \right)^{\left(\frac{1}{10} \right)} - 1 = 13.8\%$$

When collecting data, make it a habit to look through all 10 years' worth of annual report material, do not just take data from the first and last annual report. As an investor, you must be very comfortable with numbers, numbers paint a very accurate picture of a company's growth story. In addition, the research will enable the investor to have a more intimate understanding of the company that he or she is researching on. Always question the numbers and look deeper into financial years that are not of the norm, for example, a big increase or decrease in cash flow or earnings in any particular year should be researched further.

Step 2: Using CAGR, project the company's free cash

flow for the next 5 years.

Now that we have the CAGR of 13.8%, we project its yearly free cash flow for the next 5 years using the CAGR, it will be as follows

Year 2021: $12,518 (increase by 13.8% from the previous year)

Year 2022: $14,245 (increase by 13.8% from the previous year)

Year 2023: $16,211 (increase by 13.8% from the previous year)

Year 2024: $18,449 (increase by 13.8% from the previous year)

Year 2025: $20,994 (increase by 13.8% from the previous year)

Case Study

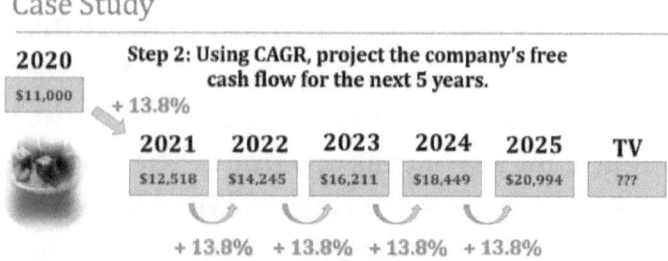

You may be asking, why project only 5 years? Why not less, say, 4 years? Or longer, maybe 10 years?

Investing is a very personal practice, you can choose the number of years you would like to forecast; if you feel that the company you are researching has a very sustainable business, by all means, increase the forecasting years. Conversely, if you feel that there may be changes in the industry that the company is in, feel free to be more conservative and forecast less. It is really, up to you. A word of caution. Forecasts are simply assumptions and forecasting further into the future may not be as meaningful. Investors usually forecast 5 years as most feel that 5 provides a good balance of accuracy and assumption.

Step 3: Calculate Terminal value.

With all this ambiguity about the future, then how do we eventually put a singular value on all these cash flows? How do we know if a business fails within a week? Or a year? Or maybe it goes on for a thousand years? Who knows?

Well, good news! The science of finance has been

able to provide a valuation model for perpetuity. Of course, it will never be 100% accurate, it does, however, give investors an estimated value on perpetual cash flows. This value is called the terminal value and it works like this.

First, we need to decide on 2 values, the discount rate and terminal growth rate. Let me explain the terminal growth rate first. We know that, from the past 10 years of data, Great Cakes have managed to compound their free cash flow at a rate of 13.8%. However, practically speaking, they are unlikely to maintain this growth rate forever. So, we will use a lesser terminal growth rate for our terminal value calculation. Let us simply use the inflation rate as our terminal growth rate, assuming Great Cakes keeps up with inflation. For the discount rate, we will use a value of 8% (to be conservative).

Terminal growth rate = 2%

Discount rate = 8%

With these 2 values, we can use the terminal value calculation formula:

[Final year cash flow x (1 + Terminal Growth Rate)] / (Discount rate – Terminal Growth rate)

The final year of cash flow is taken from year 2025: $20,994. We input the values, and this is what we'll get:

Terminal value = [$20,994 x (1 + 0.02)] / (0.08 – 0.02) = $356,898 Presto! The terminal value for Great Cakes is $356,898.

Case Study

Step 3: Calculate Terminal value. Assuming an 8% hurdle rate & a Terminal growth rate of 2% (Inflation rate)

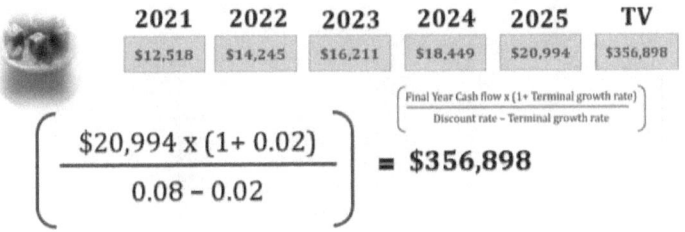

2021	2022	2023	2024	2025	TV
$12,518	$14,245	$16,211	$18,449	$20,994	$356,898

$$\left(\frac{\$20,994 \times (1 + 0.02)}{0.08 - 0.02} \right) = \$356,898 \quad \left(\frac{\text{Final Year Cash flow x (1+ Terminal growth rate)}}{\text{Discount rate – Terminal growth rate}} \right)$$

Step 4: Discount all forecasted values (including the terminal value), using the hurdle rate of 8%.

Now, we need to discount all our projected cash flows from Step 2, to get a present value of all the projected cash flows, including the terminal value.

Using the values from our present value table, the discount rate of 8% will give us the present value of all our projected cash flows:

Assuming an 8% erosion of value ...compounded.

Present Value Table

	Interest rates (r)					
4%	5%	6%	7%	8%	9%	10%
0.962	0.952	0.943	0.935	0.926	0.917	0.909
0.925	0.907	0.890	0.873	0.857	0.842	0.826
0.889	0.864	0.840	0.816	0.794	0.772	0.751
0.855	0.823	0.792	0.763	0.735	0.708	0.683
0.822	0.784	0.747	0.713	0.681	0.650	0.621
0.790	0.746	0705	0.666	0.630	0.596	0.564
0.760	0.711	0.665	0.623	0.583	0.547	0.513
0.731	0.677	0.627	0.582	0.540	0.502	0.467
0.703	0.645	0.592	0.544	0.500	0.460	0.424
0.676	0.614	0.558	0.508	0.463	0.422	0.386
0.650	0.585	0.527	0.475	0.429	0.388	0.350
0.625	0.557	0.497	0.444	0.397	0.356	0.319
0.601	0.530	0.469	0.415	0.368	0.326	0.290
0.577	0.505	0.442	0.388	0.340	0.299	0.263
0.555	0.481	0.417	0.362	0.315	0.275	0.239
0.534	0.458	0.394	0.339	0.292	0.252	0.218
0.513	0.436	0.371	0.317	0.270	0.231	0.198
0.494	0.416	0.350	0.296	0.250	0.212	0.180
0.475	0.396	0.331	0.277	0.232	0.194	0.164
0.456	0.377	0.312	0.258	0.215	0.178	0.149

Year 2021: $12,518 x 0.926 = $11,592

Year 2022: $14,245 x 0.857 = $12.208

Year 2023: $16,211 x 0.794 = $12,872

Year 2024: $18,449 x 0.735 = $13.560

Year 2025: $20,994 x 0.681 = $14,297

Do take note that the terminal value is also taken as period 5 when discounting, as we are doing the terminal value from year 2025. So that value is:

Terminal value at year 2025: $356,898 x 0.681 = $243,048

Case Study

Step 4: Discount all forecasted values (including the terminal value), using the hurdle rate of 8%.

2021	2022	2023	2024	2025	TV
$12,518	$14,245	$16,211	$18,449	$20,994	$356,898
0.926	0.857	0.794	0.735	0.681	0.681
$11,592	$12,208	$12,872	$13,560	$14,297	$243,048

Step 5: Add all the discounted values together to get the intrinsic value!

Almost there, now we add everything up, this will give us the intrinsic value of the company.

Intrinsic value = $11,592 + $12,208 + $12,872 +

$$13,560 + 14,297 + 243,048 = 307,577$$

Case Study

Step 5: Add all the discounted values together to get the intrinsic value!

	2021	2022	2023	2024	2025	TV
	$12,518	$14,245	$16,211	$18,449	$20,994	$356,898
	0.926	0.857	0.794	0.735	0.681	0.681
	$11,592	$12,208	$12,872	$13,560	$14,297	$243,048

Intrinsic value = $11,592 + $12,208 + $12,872 + $13,560 + $14,297 + $243,048 =

$307,577

Before we go into Step 6, let's put all these calculations into a stock market context. Say Great Cakes has one million shares in the market, the intrinsic value per share will be $307,577 divided by 1,000,000 shares. This will give us an intrinsic value of $0.31 per share.

Step 6: Calculate the entry price using a margin of safety.

Calculating the intrinsic value of a stock doesn't mean that we buy the stock at that price. We know that valuation models are not a 100% surety; we must make room for errors in our assumptions and calculations; hence we will use a margin of safety to determine our entry price (the price that we decide to buy the company at)

Assuming a 40% margin of safety. Your entry price will be:

$(1-0.4) \times \$0.31 = \$0.19$

This will be the price that you buy Great Cakes at. That's it! 6 simple steps to calculating the intrinsic value of a stock and setting an entry price for your investment.

Step 6: Calculate the entry price using a margin of safety.

Assuming a 40% margin of safety. Your entry price will be:

$(1-0.4) \times \$0.31 =$

$\$0.19$

Congratulations. You have officially learned how to value a stock.

CHAPTER 7

Moats

Warren Buffet first coined this term "moats" as he describes that he would much prefer to buy businesses that have a durable competitive advantage. A business with a strong and durable economic moat has 2 important characteristics. First, these businesses have strong earning power. Second, businesses with strong and durable moats possess a certain quality that is so defensive that competitors have trouble taking their market share away, similar to how a moat protects a castle from attack.

There are many different types of moats, a great value investor by the name of Phil Town, explains the differently types of moats succinctly.

Brand

People tend to buy products that are recognized

instantly and trusted by society. For instance, if you need a men's shaver, what is the first thing that comes to your mind? Gillette of course! Soft drinks? Coke! Fast food? MacDonald's. Companies that have built their brand over many years have managed to get people to link their brand to the product that they sell. Some company brands are so strong that people forget the name of the product and call the product by the brand instead! How many times have you heard someone say, "hey could you pass me a Kleenex?" When I was young, I always thought Pampers was what diapers were called, only to find out later that Pampers is a brand of diapers, in fact, it is THE brand for diapers. Now, that, is a brand moat. To consumers, great brands are related to consistent quality. People trust brands, and they are willing to pay a premium for these products, compared to a similar product with a not so strong brand image.

Switching

Everyone has bank accounts. Banks tend to offer competitive interest rates to attract depositors. If Bank A offers a higher interest rate than Bank B, why won't Bank B depositors move their funds over to Bank A instead? Inconvenience. Depositors from Bank B would have to queue up, take money out of Bank B, go to Bank A, queue up again, and open an account with Bank A, plus all the administrative and logistical matters to complete the whole transaction. Same with telecom and accounting software companies. It just takes too much time and energy to switch to another service provider, hence switching can be a very powerful moat.

Networking Effect

Companies that have a network effect moat enjoy natural monopoly. For instance, everyone uses Microsoft, be it for work, school, or play. The more users there are, the stronger the moat will be, because for daily operations to function, any sort of IT related activity for that matter, a Microsoft operating system is required. Credit card companies like American Express also enjoy a network effect moat. Merchants would only select payment process systems with the most users, as payment can be done more effectively with customers.

Toll Bridge

Companies that have a toll bridge moat are usually monopolies, most of the time having links with the country's government. For instance, utility companies. They are usually the only service provider available in a location, hence they have both market share and are price inelastic, people pay for the service no matter how much it costs. Wouldn't it be nice to own a business where customers would still buy your product even though you increase your prices? What a great moat. Media companies can also possess a toll bridge moat.

Secrets

Companies with a secrets moat usually sell products that only they can make, because, well, they have the secret formula. Kentucky fried chicken? Secret blend of herbs and spices. No one makes chicken like them. Coke? Also a secret formula. Lots of companies have their "secret" sauce on how they make their products unique, and if you can identify a company that has a great product, and no one else can manufacture them like they do, you would have found a pot of gold.

Intangible assets

Intangible assets include patents held by electronics and pharmaceutical companies (which in a way is a type of secret too!), a company with a patent is protected legally from competitors, as competitors are not allowed to produce and sell a product that is patent protected. Another intangible asset is regulatory licenses, which are really hard to attain. For more details, read up "the little book that builds wealth" by Pat Dorsey, a fabulous book for exploring economic moats.

Price

Companies with price moats are usually big retail companies which have scaled to a point where they can purchase large volumes from suppliers, giving them an edge over smaller competitors that can't get cheaper pricing from the same suppliers. With cheaper cost price per good, companies with a price moat can charge cheaper than their competitors and still be profitable. An example of a company with a price moat is Walmart.

Concluding the chapter on moats, if you can identify companies with strong and durable economic moats, wait for a price dip, buy them, and never let them go. They'll last a lifetime, and will most certainly reward you handsomely, for having a lil' faith.

FINAL WORD

There is no right or wrong in the values that you use for growth rates and discount rates. Investing is a zero-sum game, making a certain decision will have a potential opportunity cost for another decision that you chose not to make. For instance, say that you are a super conservative investor, you forecast the lowest growth rates, and use the highest discount rates in your assumptions, there is a likelihood that you will miss massive bull runs and all the insane upsides that it brings. However, the investor with the most conservative assumptions will have the most cash on hand during bear markets to snap up quality companies at dirt cheap prices. Conversely for more aggressive investors, they ride along with bull market waves and come crashing down during bear markets, as aggressive investors tend to be more generous with their purchases, they're more likely to experience big dips in their holdings from time to time (since they are more inclined to buy stocks at a higher price, compared to the conservative investor).

The price of a stock is the collective opinion of what buyers and sellers think a certain business is worth, and it's reflected in the stock market. This price changes very often because it is made up of thousands of buyers and sellers. In a sense, it is like an auction.

You must always have your own views and opinions on how much a business is worth, based on quantitative facts and qualitative insight on the business, its competitors and industry as a whole etc. You will not always be right, so be prepared to make some mistakes and lose money, but if you practice a margin of safety, you minimise your chances of being wrong.

In the end, when you invest, you must put your money where the odds are most in your favour regarding a business; what are the chances that it is likely to succeed, remain profitable and grow? This will be your best mindset to have when it comes to investing.

Ensure that you have planned out your investment horizon properly, and only use cash that you will not require in the near term. This will allow you to ride out fluctuations in the stock market, and you won't be forced to liquidate at a loss. I hope that this book has given you some basic insight on how to analyse businesses in the stock market, as a retail investor.

May your days ahead be profitable and productive! God bless.

Big Jodhi

INTRODUCTION: HOW TO ACHIEVE FINANCIAL FREEDOM

Welcome back my fellow capitalist pigs. It's time to put whatever you have learnt in the previous book into practice! What if I told you that you would only need around $230,000 to be financially secured for life? Investing is an extremely fun process, but more importantly, it must have some meaning, to you, the investor, at least. If not, why invest at all? The money that you gain must be put to some meaningful use.

Let's address the why. The why of investing. For a typical person, the term financial freedom means that one does not have to think about money every again;

to go on trips whenever one wants, to look at the left side of the menu instead of the right (where the price of this dish is usually quoted), to be able to help out a family member in need of financial aid, to give to charities, to have the freedom of choice. Money gives you choices, and this book is your path to freedom, financial freedom that is.

We'll also discuss several other ways we can earn income aside from your regular day job. So grab a cup o' Joe, sit back, relax, and let this 2nd part of "The Retail Investor" take you on a ride, a ride towards your financial freedom.

CHAPTER 1

Getting the Inspiration

P icture this. Imagine that you have enough money till the day you meet your maker. You have no worries, no obligations (aside from family), nothing. What would a typical day be like for you? Let me give you an example.

7am – Wake up.

715am – Send kids to school.

8am – Back home. Start a morning run.

830am – Freshen up. 8

45am – Laundry.

9am – Breakfast and watching the morning news/reading.

1020am – go for a movie, on your own or with your husband or wife.

1pm – Pick up kids from school.

130pm – Kids freshen up, start homework.

3pm – Kids done with homework, off to playground, shopping malls, zoo, arcade etc.

6pm – Dinner.

7pm – Quality time with family.

10pm – Bedtime.

Let's call this activity "The Freedom Exercise". Now, using this template, I would like you to personalise it. Relate it back to you. Replace it with activities that you would do when you are free of work, and of course, free of the stress of needing to earn money. Look at the list, close your eyes and envision yourself going through the activities of the day. How does it feel?

Feels great doesn't it? Without a care in the world, you do what you like, when you like. No stress, no obligation to wake up early, no frustrating morning commutes, no lunchtime crowds, no demanding bosses, no deadlines, no unhappy clients to service, nothing. Just you, and the choices that you decide to make for yourself. You do what you want to do. You are no longer a slave to money because you have enough of it! You do not have to slog it out day in day out, enduring all kinds of displeasures because you simply have no choice (unless you are ok with starving).

Now, if this exercise has stirred your soul, and you honestly desire to have a life like this, then good for you!

Let me tell you that this is possible. In fact, it's not just possible, it's an absolute certainty if you would just follow what this book says. If you want this so bad that you can taste it, even better, you WILL achieve it. What is this visceral feeling that you feel? It's desire. To be a little more specific, it's burning desire. And let me tell you my fellow capitalist pig, this is the first step towards financial freedom. You get inspired to achieve what you desire. Do yourself a favour, print out a copy of your "Freedom Exercise" and paste it in your bedroom somewhere. Make sure you read it every morning.

When you have a burning desire to achieve something, you will eventually achieve it. It just reshapes your whole outlook on life and what your purpose is.

Do you often feel that there is more to life than what you're currently doing? Most of us have routine jobs. We work without knowing why we work. We have herd mentality. My friends and family work, so, I work. Get out of that mindset. Find your purpose. Find your passion. If your passion is art, fill your freedom exercise with art activities. If your passion is underprivileged kids, fill it up with visits to orphanages. Heck, if your passion is freaking playing world of warcraft, fill it with 40-man instance raids from 7am to 7am (the next day). I don't care, as long as the thought of whatever you have on your freedom exercise gets you excited!

I'm not saying that the path to contentment is to stop working, if you love your job, by all means, continue working even after you have achieved financial freedom. The crux of the matter is, most people are not inspired by what they can achieve with money, hence they do not observe the rules of money that will inevitably get them stinking rich. To quote Dave Ramsay, getting rich is 20% mechanics and 80% behaviour. Your psychology, making wise decisions with your spending, saving, and investing, it all plays a huge part in making your ideal lifestyle come true. So what I am saying is, get a dream, a goal, an ambition of some sort, really feel it in your bones, and be disciplined on taking the steps to achieve it.

CHAPTER 2

The Money Champion

Someone told me a while back, "Big Jo, don't be so hard up about money, it can be earned back." This phrase stuck with me for a while. Can we really look at money that way? I knew I heard this phrase multiple times before, and it sickens me to know that hogwash like this is being passed on to people, and worse still, to generations after us.

You see, anyone who says this, obviously does not understand how precious money is, the blood, sweat and tears that is required when earning it, and the power that money gives its owner when put in the right place. People who utter this phrase are not champions of money, hence they don't have it. Money must be treated as precious, if not it will slip from your grasp.

So, how do we become money champions? First and foremost, Work. Find work and earn money. Aim to earn lots of it. Don't squander it though, every cent that you earn must have a destination. Ask yourself this: do you often feel that you have more "month" at the end of the "money" (your monthly wages that is)? Because you're not keeping tracking of where your money is going! Have a budget, so that you know how much you're spending, and ultimately, how much you're saving. If you don't tell your money where to go, it'll go wherever it wants to go, out of your bank account.

Next, be a business owner, not a consumer. What do I mean by this? People know Apple; they buy their products, queue up for long hours at their outlets for the latest iPhones. But chances are, none of these blokes ever thought of owning a share of Apple. In order to be a money champion, you must adopt the mind of a business owner. Use your savings to invest. Get into the stock market game. The stock market is the single greatest vehicle for all retail investors to get rich! And people are afraid of it (go figure). Stocks give the BEST returns compared to other investment classes (bonds, real estate, commodities etc.) I stress again, ignorance is poverty, and people are afraid of the stock market because they are ignorant, they do not take time to learn about it and get their feet wet into the game of investing. Instead, they choose to take the route of the consumer and buy a home (with a huge mortgage of course), a big TV and a car instead.

Poverty-minded people are consumers who love to buy things that do not generate cashflow. They accumulate useless items, or even worse, liabilities. They don't buy assets. Money champions accumulate assets that generate cashflow. Be a business owner, not a consumer.

Lastly, practice giving. Give to charities, support your religious beliefs, fund a college education for a child in a low-income family, build schools in Africa, upgrade your local libraries. Do something to benefit the people around you. When you can accumulate money, learn to give it away eventually. When the steel tycoon Andrew Carnegie died, they discovered a sheet of paper upon which he had written one of the major goals of his life; he aimed to spend the first half of his life accumulating money and to spend the last half of his life giving it all away. What a character. As money champions, we must understand that we are actually stewards of the money that we have been blessed with, and the right thing to do is to give, at least a portion of it away at some point. The single greatest joy that a human being can experience is giving, being outrageously generous to others will make you feel like a real champion. Practice giving.

CHAPTER 3

Work. Hard. Don't take your income for granted!

People love to complain about their jobs. They hate the pay. They hate the work hours. Colleagues. Bosses. Customers. Everything about their day is bad. It's really funny how people complain about being paid too little, when chances are, the value that they bring to their own workplace is mediocre at best. It's like talking to a fireplace on a cold day, "ok fire please start on your own first, when you're big enough and producing enough heat, then I'll add the wood." Seriously? Is this the mentality of our affluent middle class today? Ok my apologies, I tend to get a little cynical with people who are negative about their jobs, but honestly I just can't comprehend why people would take their jobs for granted, especially when it's their job that gives them the ability to live. it's so strange that people complain about the one thing that actually feeds them, provides for their children, entertainment, and a roof over their heads. If you are one of those that hate your job, ask yourself this: would you rather be on the streets, starving, begging? Having a job, is the single best thing that any human being can have. A job gives you a form of social standing and brand about yourself, and it keeps you busy, while making you money at the same time. Then why do people often hate their jobs? It boils down to the same issue discussed in the previous chapter, inspiration. Motivation towards a worthwhile goal.

So, there are many reasons why people dislike their jobs. It can be the nature of work, handling unreasonable customers, toxic work environment, demanding bosses, or a supposedly meagre compensation. Two ways you can solve this for yourself.

Solution 1. Leave the darn job. It actually speaks more about your own insecurity and self-worth when you stick to a job that you hate, because you are the one contributing to all the negativity not only in your mind, but to others as well. Consider what is a deal breaker for you to leave your job. Write down a list of things that you like about your job, and a list of things that you hate about your job. If you find that there are issues that really just make you sick, make a firm decision to leave it, and search for something better. Be wise about it though, you're risking your entire livelihood on this decision. Make sure you have a backup plan.

Solution 2. Change your mindset and perspective about your job. Similar to the first solution, do up a list of likes and dislikes about your current job. Find out the things that motivate you about your job. Be thankful for those positive pointers. And, for things that you are unhappy about, find ways to shift your mindset to look at these negative pointers in a different light, or better still, find solutions to turn the negative pointers into not so negative ones. For instance, if your department is particularly toxic, you can avoid the toxic co-workers or request a shift to another department. If your customers are unreasonable, find ways to go out of your way to service them, satisfy them, and amaze them with your customer service. You'd be surprised how an unhappy customer can be turned into your greatest fan. If you have demanding superiors, try and understand that they have deadlines and requirements that they're trying to fulfil. Ask yourself this question: what is my superior's KPI/ goal/ objective and how do I help him or her achieve it? Or how do I make my superior's job easier? To help him or her worry less about the department. Pivot your behaviours, actions and thinking towards this angle and you will almost certainly have a much easier time with your superiors. Easier said than done though, then again, nothing worthwhile doing comes easy.

To put things plainly, if you would just put in 110% effort in everything you do at work (easier said than done, I get it, but you have to put in the effort if you want to enjoy the good things in life), serving your clients, customers, and superiors, you will have a much easier time at work. Why? Because you are bringing value to people around you. When you get recognised for being a person that adds value to anyone you're interacting with, you will receive social, and financial recognition; your pay will be directly correlated to the value that you bring to the table. You'd naturally feel better about yourself and your work as well.

Don't wish for things to get easier, instead, wish that you become better at what you do, increase your capacity, and things will get easier in the long run. Don't be lazy about work. Even the simplest job will bring in money, and remember, with every dime you collect and save, you can potentially bring in more nickels and dimes through investing (more of this in our later chapters). Never look down on any kind of work. And never, ever, take your existing job for granted. Work your tail off. Nothing beats the satisfaction of a hard day of fulfilling work.

CHAPTER 4

Save. As much you can!

Do you find yourself being constantly out of money before the month ends? How does that make you feel?

I remembered when I was in my 20s, still living with my parents, I would spend my months' wages in 2 weeks, and then going to my mum for extra money. It made me feel lousy because I felt so dependent and irresponsible, and I was irresponsible. The feeling of not having money is horrible. I eventually decided to change my ways and became more disciplined in saving. It has done wonders. I feel happier about myself and I don't feel the guilt that I used to feel for being so loose with my wages.

One problem that I faced was not knowing where my money went, it just seemed to disappear without me knowing. So, as I listened to Dave Ramsay (please Google him if you don't know who I'm talking about, this man is a personal finance guru), he said that every-one MUST have a written budget, and stick to it. Now, budgets are tough to maintain, chances are, we would not follow the budgets that we create. So maybe, let's take a baby step 0.5, instead of the usual baby steps from the Financial Peace University. Instead of doing a Budget, start by tracking all your expenses first. Track them for a month. Every single penny. At the end of the month, go through your list of expenses and you'll have a revelation on how much money you're actually wasting, whether it's on five dollar lattes from Starbucks, or a subscription service that you hardly use, like a gym membership or Netflix. Then slowly start cutting from there. Take note of the total amount of expenses that you cut, and with that, add a final expense, title it "pay yourself first." That's the tax that you're going to put on your total salary for the month. This is the way to get rich. A part of all you earn is yours to keep. Save, and the next chapter will show you how you can invest your way to finan-cial freedom later, using the savings that you have ac-cumulated. I use an app called Wally to track my ex-penses, it's really useful, I'd recommend downloading that app on your smart phone for tracking expenses.

It's definitely a sacrifice to reduce your standard of living, at least for a while. I understand. It's tough to let go of all these luxuries. It's just too painful and demoralising, living below your means. If you really can't bring yourself to cutting down your expenses, my only advice is, to work hard at your job and increase your value there. Otherwise, getting financially secure is really just a pipe dream for you. Nothing worth doing comes easy. And if you're willing to make the sacrifice, you'll enjoy the fruits of your labour in time to come.

CHAPTER 5

The Freedom Fund

The term "financial freedom" gets thrown around a lot. I won't be surprised if it actually scares some people. This absolute number that is so big that most of us think it's unattainable. What do you think that number is? 1 million? 2 million? Suze Orman says the number is 10 million dollars, to retire comfortably. No wonder people are giving up and spending like children. Let me give you some hope. It's not. In fact, it's way smaller than you think it actually is. With the right strategy and mindset, you too can reach a basic level of financial freedom, most of the time, way before official retirement age.

Let's analyse the two words "financial freedom". It literally means free from financial obligations. So, in your own life, what are your financial obligations? I'm talking about needs here, not wants. Let's break it down and list the order of importance. 1 being the most important of course.

1. Mortgage/rent
2. Food and water
3. Utilities
4. Transportation
5. Insurance

These are your 5 main expenses that you need to cover to at least live decently. So, if you can find a way to generate enough income passively (we'll explain this in our later chapters) that can cover all the 5 main expenses, then technically, you are financially secure! So first things first, let's figure out those monthly expense numbers. Use your Wally app to help you with this. I'll use my own personal expenses as an example.

1. Mortgage/rent - $1,200
2. Food and water - $500
3. Utilities - $100
4. Transportation - $140
5. Insurance - $60

Add those expenses up and you get a whopping $2,000 a month in basic expenditure. $24,000 a year.

Now, we need a freedom fund. This fund will buy you out of slavery, slavery from financial obligations that is. This is the total amount of capital that you must accumulate, through savings and investments, that would allow you to yield a passive income of $24,000 annually, without having you physically working for it. Before I forget, let me share that there are 3 main types of income:

Active income – any type of income that requires your time, presence, availability, and energy. This is usually your job. You are trading time for money. This is the worst type of income to rely on.

Portfolio income – any type of income that comes from investments. Dividends and capital gains are some examples of portfolio income.

Passive income – any type of income that does not require you managing it. The income flows to you automatically. An example would be a private business that you have built up and others are running the business for you. You're not required to manage it and still get income from it.

Ok, good that we got that out of the way. This book mainly talks about portfolio income, and a little bit of passive income as well, but we'll come to that later. First, please think about your yearly expenses number ready before reading the next paragraph.

The great motivational speaker and financial guru Tony Robbins explains the freedom fund concept very clearly in one of his YouTube videos; search for "Tony Robbins tap the power", his video should pop up. I would also highly recommend anyone to get a copy of two of his books "Money: master the game" and "unshakeable". these two books changed my life (apart from rich dad poor dad).

According to Tony Robbins, there are 3 levels of financial freedom:

Financial security - this first stage is where basic necessities are covered. Passive income from your freedom fund covers basic expenses.

Financial independence - this second stage includes having everything else covered. A good benchmark for this is when your passive income is the same as your salary.

Financial freedom - this is the final stage, where you literally can't outspend your freedom fund. Everything you can think of is covered by your passive income.

Sounds awesome doesn't it? I hope you're motivated by this. Let's not get over the top here, we'll first set a goal to hit level 1, which is financial security. $24,000 is my number, I hope you have yours. Let's go on to the next chapter to see how we can achieve this.

CHAPTER 6

Invest in the Stock Market. Go all in!
Compound interest

The stock market is the single most effective vehicle to grow your wealth safely and steadily. In my previous book, "The Retail Investor: How to Analyse Businesses in the Stock Market", I go into the nitty gritty of analysing financial statements and how to make practical stock purchases. Do yourselves a favour and grab a copy of it too.

Anyway, back to the stock market. Contrary to popular belief, the stock market is actually NOT risky. However, you must have these 3 requirements.

Holding power

Have holding power for your stock market investments. The stock market has returned on average between 8~10% in total investment returns historically. This percentage, however, is averaged out through 50 to 70 years. Some years it can earn as much as 30% and some years it can go down as much as 90% (read up on stock market performance during the Great Depression in the 1930s). When deciding on how much of your savings you want in the stock market, always consider funds that you know for sure that you won't need to use for at least the next 5-10 years. You don't want to be caught "Swimming naked in the sea when the tide goes out", having to liquidate your portfolio of stock market investments during a recession or a bear market season. Stocks are super volatile in the short term, but we always know where the stock market goes in the long term, it goes up. Why? Because of human potential, productivity, innovation and of course an increase in population as well. Human beings need goods and service to live, what are the chances that 10-15 years from now the global economic machine will produce less than today? Unless of course a comet hits the earth, or an all-out nuclear war. When that happens, I think your best investment would be buying an eBook on how to hunt for food effectively.

Diversify

Tell me something. Is it logical to put all your savings into a single company? There was once a hand phone company, called Nokia. When I was in school, every kid owned at least a Nokia 3310 (those bulky handphones that could stop a bus). They were very clearly the dominant players in the mobile phone industry. At their peak, they probably earned about 4 billion in profits. Where are they now? Acquired by Microsoft. Sad. From being the dominant mobile phone company, to losing their market value from a high of about 25 euros per share in 2007 to less than 2 euros in 2013. A 92% decline in value. Imagine if you were to dump all your savings of say $50,000 in your the "sure win" investment, Nokia, you would have lost $46,000, with no recovery in sight. So, when you purchase stocks, always make sure you do your research, and buy at least 8-10 companies if you're confident. Alternatively, just index. I'll explain more on this later in the chapter.

No such thing as get rich quick

If you have a gambler's mentality to get rich quick, stay out of the stock market. Your greed and lack of knowledge will lead you to make dumb purchases based on seemingly hot (actually scammy) stock tips. If there's one thing to understand about the laws of wealth, it is that to attain a lot of wealth, you must have a rich mindset (money champion), and money champions with the rich mindset know that getting rich quick is a myth. Legendary motivational speaker Jim Rohn once said that if you take all the money in the world, divide it up equally among everybody, eventually the money will still end up back in the same pockets. Why is this so? Because every individual has a certain wealth mindset. If you have a rich mindset, you'll be rich. If you have a poverty mindset, no matter how much money you get your hands on, you're bound to lose all of it eventually. There are countless cases of celebrities, Star Athletes, lottery winners who hit it big time and make a ton of money at one point of their lives, only to lose it all eventually. Johnny Depp, Francis Ford Coppola, Mike Tyson, just to name a few. Getting rich quick does not exist, don't think that a stock will shoot up 1000% within a few days. Don't gamble. And for goodness sake, don't get me started on bitcoin.

Alright sorry for the sermon. I digress. Back to investing.

As you all know, I'm a major proponent of the stock market investing. Whether or not you pick individual stocks, mutual funds, or ETFs, doesn't really matter, as Long as you get into the game of stock market investing. Now here's another concept that needs no introduction: compound interest.

Let me tell you the story of two friends, William and James. William starts investing at 23, the age that he starts working. He puts away $500 dollars a month ($6,000 annually) and does this for 10 years, stops at 33, and just leaves it in the stock market to grow (8% compounded). The table below shows how much he accumulated over the years till he hits 65.

William	
Age	**Freedom Fund**
23	6,000
24	12,480
25	19,478
26	27,037
27	35,200
28	44,016
29	53,537
30	63,820
31	74,925
32	86,919
33	93,873
65	**1,101,794**

James does the exact same thing, but he starts at age 35 instead, and he continues to save and invest all the way till he reaches 65. Let's see how much he has at 65.

James			
Age	Freedom Fund	Age	Freedom Fund
35	6,000	51	202,501
36	12,480	52	224,701
37	19,478	53	248,678
38	27,037	54	274,572
39	35,200	55	302,538
40	44,016	56	332,741
41	53,537	57	365,360
42	63,820	58	400,589
43	74,925	59	438,636
44	86,919	60	479,726
45	99,873	61	524,105
46	113,863	62	572,033
47	128,972	63	623,796
48	145,290	64	679,699
49	162,913	65	**740,075**
50	181,946		

As seen in both tables, not only did William accumulate substantially more money than James ($361,000 more to be exact, almost 50% more), but he also did it with less capital. William saved a grand total of $6000 x 10 years = $60,000, while James saved a grand total of $6000 x 30 years = $180,000. So let's sum up, William puts in less money than James and still has more than his friend when he retires at 65! The critical difference was starting earlier! Time is the most important element in compound interest.

So let's look back at our own expense numbers, shall we? We know how much we earn per month, we know how much we spend, which leads to knowing how much we save. We know our number for financial security, we know how compounding interest works. Let's discuss the type of stock investment vehicle we can put our monthly savings in.

Typically, the simplest method is to automate your savings to buy an index fund. Preferably from the country that you live in, if you're a US citizen, S&P 500 or DJIA index fund or ETF will do the trick, if you're English, it's footsie. If you're Aussie, ASX. An index fund or a market index ETF buys the top companies in the countries of your choosing, and they bundle it up to make it a single stock; you save money on the brokers fees, management fees and you get diversification. In addition, market indices beat most fund managers who pick stocks. In other words, for all the quants and hedge fund managers out there who charge ludicrous fees for their "investment expertise", they actually don't beat a simple index fund or an index ETF over the long term, so, indexing is the way to go.

Now, there are two methods that you can pay for your financial security stage using your freedom fund. The first method to is to slowly sell off a piece of the freedom fund annually, so that you have liquidity for your expenses. Typically, a recommended amount would be 4 percent annually. The good thing about this method is that you don't have to save as much money compared to the 2nd method which I'm going to share with you shortly. The downside of the first method is that you slowly eat away into your principal, which means you have to really plan and watch your budget properly, to ensure that you have cash flow for as long as you live.

So how big must my freedom fund be for method 1?

25 x $24,000 = $600,000.

This method is called FIRE (Financial independence retire early). The FIRE concept emphasises on aggressive savings. So, according to FIRE, if you can save 75% of your income, you can technically be financially secure in less than 10 years. If you're 30 and reading this, it means that you can be financially secure by 40!

The second method is to live off the dividends of your freedom fund. Typically, index funds give about 2-3 percent in dividends annually, so your freedom fund number must actually be around 30 to 50 times your annual expenses, compared to the first method where you only need say around 25 times your annual expenses. Let's use my personal expenses number of $24,000 again.

If my investments yield 2% in dividends, the freedom fund would be 50 x $24,000 = $1.2 million.

If my investments yield 3% in dividends, the freedom fund would be 30 x $24,000 = $720,000.

Similar to FIRE, a high savings rate will fast track your financial goals. Obviously.

Now, the second method may seem daunting, but remember that companies grow in profits, and dividends will likely increase as the years go by. If you can, put aside as much money as you can into investing, especially if you're still in your twenties, it will be the best decision of your life. Go for the 2nd method of investing, yes, it'll take longer, but it'll also last a lot longer as your principal amount/ freedom fund is left totally untouched.

CHAPTER 7

Other forms of income

N ow that we know what our freedom fund number is, being financially secure doesn't seem that impossible now does it? It is relatively far away, I'm sure most of us will take at least 10-12 years. But at the very least there is light at the end of the tunnel.

For those of you weird people who are even more determined to reach your financial objectives faster, there are only 2 options: reduce your expenses, or earn more money. Plain and simple. The best profession to increase income quickly is a salesperson, the sky is the limit for the salesperson if he or she is effective. If you're in a sales job, I hope that this book gives you the motivation and hunger that you need to close more deals. For those of us with fixed wages, do not fear. There are avenues that we can increase our income, other than through our job promotions. Here are some practical ways to give a boost to your income.

The Internet

The internet age has given us the opportunity to make untold amounts of money. Just Google Ryan Kaji. He is the highest paid kid YouTube Star, generating $22 million dollars in 2018. What does he do on his YouTube channel Ryan Toysreview? His dad simply films him playing and unboxing toys! Sounds simple? Certainly. Ryan had 17 million followers in 2018. The power of the internet has allowed so much influence and connectivity globally, that starting online businesses become so simple to start and lucrative at the same time.

YouTube

YouTube is a great platform for earning side income. Think of it as sort of a tv station, run by a single person, the youtuber. The image of the channel, video content, filming, editing, and posting can all be done by a single person. A YouTuber would set up a channel, post interesting videos on his or her channel, attract as many viewers as possible and hopefully convert them to subscribers. Then, when the channel grows to at least 1000 subscribers, with 4000 hours of watch time within the span on a year, the channel can be monetized by YouTube. This means that, because the channel has a good chunk a regular viewers, it would worthwhile for YouTube to place ads on the videos posted by that channel. The value of a channel is largely dependent on the number of subscribers it has. And, once the channel gets monetized, guess who gets a cut of the ad revenue collected? The youtuber of course! YouTube is a video distribution site, but ultimately its main goal is to get as many users as possible, in turn attracting massive human traffic, and for any platform that has loads of human traffic, it means that the platform itself is fertile ground for companies to market their products and services. This is how Ryan the kid youtuber made so much money. Of course, not all of his earnings was ad revenue, but I'm sure at some point in his YouTube career, it was. Do you think 22 million dollars paid out was a big sum for YouTube? I doubt so, they must have earned tons more from the companies who paid them to place ads in the first place! I'd highly recommend giving YouTube a try. Think of something that you enjoy doing. Fishing? Cooking? Playing games? Shopping? These are all pretty interest topics to build video content around. Let's say that you enjoy eating great food and you spend your weekends hunting for great eateries and restaurants. Instead of just simply eating, get a GoPro ready and do a video review on the dishes! You'd be surprised at how much fun it actually is making videos and posting them, especially if it is something that you have a passion for. Find your niche. Paired up with passion. You'll find yourself hooked to creating videos.

Of course, it is easier said than done, getting your YouTube channel monetized. There must be a lot of thought and time invested into the channel and video content, to really make it quality videos for viewers to enjoy. One critical factor to understand is the almighty YouTube algorithm, the system that decides if your video is worth being pushed to viewers. Search engine optimisation strategies must be implemented by the Youtuber as well, to help boost video searches.

Tons of work is required to build a successful channel, which is why the first question that you must answer for yourself is, that the niche that you decide to do videos about must be your passion. You have to enjoy doing it. If not, it will be chore for you to produce videos regularly.

Take your time with it. I'm not a YouTuber, but I sure am inspired by successful YouTubers and I follow a good number of them. One of my favourites is Graham Stephan. He is a real estate agent/ investor/ YouTuber, and his topics are always about money, investments, and personal finance. As of this year 2020, he has roughly 2.28 million subscribers. Back in 2019 he made a video about how much money he made on YouTube with 1 million subscribers, it was a whopping 1.2 million dollars. Now he is nowhere close to Ryan toysreview, but the reason why I enjoy his content so much is because he constantly brings his viewers back to when he first started putting videos on YouTube, how he started recording videos using just his iPhone, and how he grew his channel at a very gradual pace. He always said that he never did it for the money, but rather, he did it because he enjoyed sharing video content that he was passionate about. Lo and behold, this simple reason has led him to where his today in his YouTube standing. 2.28 million people tune in to listen to him rant about finance matters 3 times a week; think of all the ads that is constantly being flashed at his viewers, and the disgusting amounts of money that Mr Stephan is making, while he literally does nothing. Nothing at all.

Like most passive income strategies, it usually takes a huge amount of work, time, and energy to build the source of income before being able to actually see and enjoy the income. YouTubers can literally be pretty much hands off from the channel once it takes off (although most get even more motivated to produce more content). Mr Stephan did mention that he still makes ad revenue money from videos that he posted years ago, and that should he decide to stop making videos altogether, he would still be able to generate income from his older videos.

Affiliate marketing

Now, this ties in greatly with YouTube. So, let's say you start a YouTube channel reviewing audio equipment, and you managed to garner a good number of subscribers and you have a decent following. You can actually help these audio equipment companies with their marketing efforts, by doing a positive review for the equipment, and leaving a link or a discount code in your description. When people buy through your affiliate link, you get a small commission from the sale! A common affiliate programme to join is Amazon Associates; simply sign up for an account, choose the products that you would be reviewing, create an Amazon Affiliate link and presto! You are officially an affiliate.

Search engine optimisation

Let's talk a little about search engines. All big E commerce companies run on search engines; Google, yahoo, amazon, Alibaba etc. These search engines serve a fundamental need - to bring a relevant product/ service to a customer that is ready to purchase. This is why E commerce is so powerful. There is no more need for customers to physically hunt for any desired product. Just simply type in the search box and the search engine will find the item for you.

Rankings and keyword searches

With that in mind, how E commerce businesses make their money, is by first optimising their product search through rankings. E commerce businesses list their products online, inputting common keywords that people search for, and linking those keywords to their products. The search engine will then match the keyword relating to their product. The prospective buyer will click on their links, and they'll eventually be led to the product landing page where they can purchase the desired product or service.

Internet advertising

So, how does a company ensure that their website or

product page is listed as the rank #1 in a search result? Well, they first need to make tons of sales to tell the search engine algorithm that the product is indeed relevant and saleable. Sounds like an tough fight right? Imagine a fresh company trying to compete with older companies with an E commerce presence? There's little or no chance that the new company can appear at rank #1 on the search result. This is where internet advertising comes in.

For instance, tech and E commerce giants Amazon and Google provide advertising services and charge users based on clicks. Let me explain how this works.

Impressions

Say a new company engages Amazon to market their products, what Amazon does is to put the company's product link in front of users as an advertisement. This is called an impression, since the user will see the advertisement. Amazon will only charge the company if the user clicks on the advertisement, whether or not the company buys the product is not Amazon's problem anymore; they have successfully directed customer traffic To the company's product page/ website. The rest of the work is up to the company's/ individual's ad copy (a sales letter that features the benefits of the product).

This is generally how internet advertising cost structure works; cost per click.

Ad copy

Now, this is like a product description, it applies to all E Commerce products and video distribution companies like YouTube (for YouTube, it's slightly different, content creators use thumbnails and compelling video titles to attract people to click on their links). It is like a product description, or a link description that compels a prospective customer to buy the product, or click on the link to watch the content in the video. Mastering ad copy is a powerful skill for individuals who want to succeed in online businesses.

E Commerce

Now this is interesting. Remember how when we wanted something in the past, we would need to go the physical store to actually buy our desired product? We go to a particular retail store, right? Not anymore. With the rise of E commerce, online retail stores are the new kids in town in the merchandising game. Blame it on Amazon and Alibaba. Or.. China, whichever way you want to spin this blame game.

Drop shipping

Think of how the old school supply chain management used to work. There are manufacturers, and retailers. The retailers would source products from the manufacturers, buy the goods wholesale, get a good discount for making a bulk purchase, store it in their warehouses and ship the goods out to all their retail outlets. The products would then be displayed in the retail storefront to entice customers to purchase their products. Now with E commerce, we can do away with the physical store presence. Why? Because human traffic has gone online! Furthermore, payment modes have become so much more convenient than say,10-15 years ago, there is really not much reason why customers should take the trouble to go out of their homes, into the malls and stores to buy products. They can simply go on a shopping spree from their own homes.

With this new culture, E commerce retail stores start to emerge; online retail stores that display items for sale via their websites. So now, wait a minute, Remember the whole supply chain process that was described earlier? Numerous agencies and tons of staff are required to work together to make the whole supply chain operation work. So then, how is one person going to run the whole supply chain operations? Won't the products need to be stored in warehouses; orders matched to customers addresses etc.? What about sourcing for manufacturers? Won't a whole team of merchandisers be required for that?

All valid questions, and all these questions can be solved, by engaging the services of an E commerce platform company.

Shopify

Shopify is an E commerce platform that helps online retailers set up an online store and sell their products. They provide a basic template your online store website, you can design it, beautify it, put useful instructional videos and tips on the products that you are selling. Shopify also handles all the warehousing, order tracking and even providing manufacturers and suppliers to its users. Shopify's business model is primarily a subscription service, so its users pay an annual fee to use all its resources and of course to get back end support as well.

Oberlo

Oberlo is a subsidiary of Shopify, and their main task is to facilitate the importing of products from retailers to customers, they handle all the logistics and warehousing. Best of all, the retailer bears no inventory risk! Back in the day, conventional retailers had to buy a ton of inventory to get a bulk discount, however, the risk was that the retailer would not know if he or she could sell all the product that was bought. In this day and age, with E commerce, the inventory is bought only when an order comes in. Oberlo handles this. They act as the middleperson linking manufacturers with retailers, who would then ultimately provide for the customers. Guess who their biggest supplier is? China! Or AliExpress. China is known as the world's factory because they can produce goods at a fraction of the costs of manufacturers in other parts of the world. Oberlo has direct links to AliExpress, if I'm not mistaken, all their products are from AliExpress. So, all the online retailer has to do is to source for customers! Drive traffic to their online retail store, or Shopify store. Products are so cheap that the retailer can mark up its retail price to 3 or 4 times its purchase cost!

The online retail business can be very lucrative, and the work involved is considerably less than conventional retail, and on top of that, everything can be done at home! Who knew that buying and selling products could be done in the comfort of your own home! By just one person!

Fulfilment by Amazon (FBA)

FBA is a similar E commerce business model. But, instead of having an online store, the sellers simply list their products in the Amazon universe. Amazon gives the retailer access to millions of customers.

So how exactly does FBA work, first, have a product to sell. Then, package the products according to the specifications that Amazon requires, and you simply send your prepared products to the Amazon fulfilment centres. These centres will settle the distribution to your buyers (the people who are buying your products through Amazon). Do take note that there are fulfilment fees and inventory storage fees involved in this particular business venture.

Self-published author

If you're someone who is knowledgeable about a topic, I would suggest that you get cracking on a book! Or an eBook. The book that you're reading now, took 7 days to get created. Best of all, it's free! You do not have to sink a ton of capital into inventory, or the physical publishing of the book itself, and finding a vendor to display your book. I'll get into the nitty gritty of publishing later. But first, let me share with you my story.

I have been obsessed with personal finance and the stock market since 2015. I devoured countless books on investments even till this day and will continue to be avid reader for the days to come. I just love reading so much. It expands my mind intellectually and psychologically as well. I constantly get inspired from these books. What better way to make a small impact to the world by penning down your knowledge into writing! From the time I started seriously reading, I probably read more than 200 books. My knowledge on investing became pretty extensive, and I soon found myself becoming the go to person in my workplace when it came to money, investments, and personal finance. It feels great to be known for a particular niche.

So one day, I finally decided to write a book. 3 months later, I published "The Retail Investor: How to Analyse Businesses in the Stock Market" on KDP.

So, what is KDP?

Kindle Direct Publishing (KDP)

Amazon developed an electronic reading device some time back called Kindle, and this device stores eBooks sold by Amazon. It's like the iPod (a device to store music tracks), but instead of storing music, the kindle stores eBooks that the user purchases. With kindle, you can download eBooks directly from the machine itself. Pretty cool.

Of course, with an eBook platform, amazon had to come up with a self-publishing service as well. Kindle direct publishing (KDP) was launched together with kindle in 2007. Now, indie authors can independently publish their books and sell them online via the kindle store.

Writing a book may seem like a daunting task. It can be tiring, but it's not as difficult as you think. As always, you first need to be passionate about a subject. Then pen the chapter titles down so that you have a basic idea about what you would like to write with regards to that topic. Next, discipline yourself to write at least 500 to 1000 words at a certain time of the day. As you write, you'll get a momentum and snowball effect with your ideas. Before you know it, you'll be jotting down furiously because your typing speed can't keep up with your ideas! Trust me on this. Put it in a word document, format it nicely (just YouTube how to format an eBook) and upload your manuscript onto your KDP account. The initial set up is really easy and the instructions are simple to understand as well. Give it a try! You may already have material for a bestseller, you just don't know it yet.

So, how do authors earn money? Royalties of course!

Once your book is in the Amazon market, the sky is the limit. Amazon makes payment so easy for users, and eBooks are significantly cheaper compared to physical books (price range is usually 2.99-9.99) so customers are more inclined to just buy the book to see what it's all about. As your book gains popularity (by purchases and reviews), the Amazon algorithm will feature your books even more to potential customers, and a virtuous cycle will take place, enabling you to earn even more book sales. And did I forget to mention, all this is complete passive? Initial work done is tough, but once your book is published, you can just sit back, relax, and let Amazon do the heavy lifting for you regarding marketing and promotion.

Another interesting feature of KDP is that once your book is published, KDP will automatically opt your book into KDP select. This special programme gets the book enrolled into Kindle unlimited, a book subscription service provided by Kindle. On top of the royalties that you get from book purchases, Amazon will also pay you per page read from the any user who borrows your book through kindle unlimited! How's that for awesome!? Ok, it's slightly less than half a cent per page. But if you gain more popularity and more readership, over time these pages can really add up. it's really meant to supplement your book sale royalties. You get income from online book purchases and pages read by borrowers. Let's get into a hypothetical situation. Say you wrote a book for 3.99 USD, and you get a book purchase every other day (remember that Amazon has hundreds of millions of users, so your book is potentially exposed to that amount of traffic), that's already almost 60 USD. Add on having 5 readers finish your book via kindle unlimited every day, that's another 60 USD (5 people x 100 pages x 30 days). That's a whole 120 USD every month, 1440 USD at the end of the year! And all this is being earned without you having to spend any more time on it, apart from the initial phase of writing and publishing the book.

I know, I make it sound like it's too good to be true. It's not impossible, but it's not easy as well, to get your book popular in Amazon. That's why further research is needed on how you can use better search optimisation strategies (similar to YouTube) so that your book will appear higher on the ranking page when users search for the topic that you wrote about. In addition, you need to hire a graphic designer to design a beautiful book cover for your book, and of course, write a compelling description for your book as well.

Publishing a great book and getting book sales off the ground is one asset that is so worth creating because the income generation at the end is just so passive.

Real estate

Now this is a big one. Real estate investing has been around for the longest time, and people make tons of money on buying and selling houses. More importantly, if you're going to venture into real estate for passive income, it would be wiser to focus on the steady rental income that it yields. This type of income is slightly different from the internet business though. A ton of capital is required for a real estate purchase, so you need to actually save up for a year or two before deciding to take the plunge. Of course you absolutely have to educate yourself on real estate investing! Pop by the library and devour any real estate book that you can find. Learn the ropes first. Don't blindly go to one open house and make a purchase on the spot. You are putting a lot of money at stake.

A reason why people get into real estate is that the property itself is tangible, and it solves a very essential need, shelter. Everybody needs a roof over their heads, and if you own a property, you can almost be certain that there will be a demand for it. The wealthiest people in the world own tons of properties. Donald Trump made his fortune in real estate. Robert Kiyosaki. Robert Kuok. Lee Ka-Shing. Barbara Corcoran. Grant Cardone, Mochtar Riady. These are all real estate moguls.

Another reason that real estate investing is so popular, is the leverage that it provides. Obviously, for the average middle-class worker, we will take many years to pay for a house fully in cash, we need to utilise debt to get into the game of real estate. Thankfully, banks are willing to lend money to make real estate purchases.

For any investor, the number one metric to determine if an investment is worthwhile is this, Return on Investment, or ROI. How much returns can I get, as the investor, off my initial capital outlay (principal) on a yearly basis? So, let's use a hypothetical scenario. Say you found an awesome apartment for $800,000, and the rental yield is $3,000 per month. This would make up an annual yield of 4.5% (12 months X $3,000 rental = $36,000, which makes up 4.5% of $800,000). Not too juicy right? If you were to save up $800,000 cash to purchase the apartment, that would be your yield. At 4.5%, you could have dollar cost averaged into an index ETF from day 1 of saving the $800k, and letting compound interest for you, rather than to save up for 5-7 years, letting the money sit in the back at less than 0.05% interest. The opportunity cost for saving the full payment of the apartment would be too much to bear. This is where the bank comes in. As a buyer, you can enlist the help of your bank to fund at least 80% of your purchase price, and you only need to come up with 20% as your capital outlay. Let's do some maths.

Purchase price of apartment: $800,000

Mortgage: 80% of $800,000 = $640,000

Your capital outlay: 20% of $800,000 = $160,000

See! With the help of a bank, you only need to come up with $160,000, a quarter of what you initially had to come up with. Now, this is where it gets juicy. Check it out.

Say the bank charges 3% interest on the mortgage, which makes up to an annual interest expense of $19,200 (3% X $640k X 12 months). We also know that we can yield $24,000 annually from rental income.

Annual rental income = $36,000

Annual interest expense = $19,200

Annual cashflow from apartment = $36,000 - $19,200 = $16,800.

Now, this $16,800 cashflow is your ROI. What is $16.8k of $160k? That is a 10.5% cash on cash return! This phenomenon is called leverage in the finance world. People get into real estate because of leverage.

Before you dis my simplistic example, yes there are other factors and expenses that come into play here, like maintenance costs, advertising for tenants etc. The point that I'm trying to get across is that with real estate, you can really get a boost in your returns as you have an ally to help you, the bank. At 10.5% return, you can double your money in less than 7 years. Amazing right?

Real estate is the bomb. It's one of the most exciting ways to build wealth. Relating back to our financial security numbers, calculate how much capital you would actually need to hit the target. Say you have learnt the ways of real estate and you are experienced enough to get great real estate deals that yield 10.5% cash every year. If your total yearly expenses is $24,000, you technically only need less than $230,000 to be financially secure! How's that for an "alternative" source of income?

Let's talk a little bit about the capital appreciation part. If the apartment were to increase its value by $800,000, the new price of the apartment would be $880,000. Let's see how much money the investor makes from the sale.

Cash received from sale of apartment: $880,000

Return the loan: $640,000

Residual cash: $880,000-$640,000 = $240,000

Initial capital outlay: $160,000

Capital appreciation: $(240,000-160,000)/160,000 = a whopping 50% increase in capital appreciation!

See the power of leverage? You only needed the apartment to increase its value by 10% to get an actual 50% cash on cash capital appreciation, on top of the years of collecting a 10.5% annual rental yield. An obscene amount of money can potentially be made in real estate.

A word of caution: never over-lever. Debt is double edged sword, if you use it wisely you can augment your overall returns, if you use excessively, it will complete decimate your wealth. Always consider the fact that there will be times that tenants are hard to find, and that your property may be vacant, while still having the obligation to pay the mortgage expense. Don't let your real estate by the banks.

Part time work for special services

What do you do on the weekends? Anything productive? Chances are, you would be partying with friends, getting wasted and watching Netflix. Why not do something useful? When I was in my teenage years, I was fortunate enough to use my other skills to earn income. I was a music teacher, and I got paid $20 an hour to teach music to young kids. I worked on Friday evenings and the whole of Saturday. Bear in mind that I was around 18-19 years old back then. I was pulling an average of $600 per month! Not too shabby for an alcoholic teen, right? Unfortunately, I was too dumb back then to save, and I blew it all on parties and liquor. What I'm trying to say here is, when you have spare time on your hands, make it a point to spend some of your free hours working part time! There must be another skill that you're good at! Do a cooking class, be a swimming coach. Personal trainer. I see a lot of people in great shape, but I doubt they do any private training. Give private maths tuition to struggling youngsters. Do something that can earn you some extra income. Remember, capitalise on your youth to work your tail off, so that when you get older, you can reap the fruits of your labour. Imagine your freedom fund starting off as a seedling, and you water it, nourish, in time it will grow into a tree, and you can bask in its shade.

CHAPTER 8

Generosity.

Congratulations on reaching the end of this book. With the knowledge you have now, I'm certain that you would be able to achieve financial freedom in the years to come. Let's explore the choices you can have once you have financial freedom.

Settling essential expenses easily

With the passive income that you have, you do not have to worry for another day in your life that you won't be able to afford water, electricity, and food. It's all taken care of by your freedom fund.

Entertainment is almost unlimited

If you choose to work even after achieving financial freedom, you will have tons more liquidity to do the things that you enjoy. It's almost to a point where, you can recklessly spend your money on a short holiday every month, and not even make a dent on your salary. You wouldn't even need to use your earned income. Imagine that. Or, if you have that dream car that you always wanted to buy, you can simply save the income that comes from your freedom fund and make the purchase with those savings. It would look a little strange though, if say you were a simple schoolteacher and you own a Jaguar (people might think you peddle heroine on the side, sorry for bad joke, I kid).

Setting aside funds for kids college

For those of you capitalist pigs with piglets to support, your freedom fund can buy your kids a good education. Don't tell them that though, you don't want them to take their privileges for granted.

Helping family with health issues

Healthcare costs are constantly rising. Wouldn't it be a relief to be able to pick up the bill for an ailing family member? Or even for yourself (touch wood), if you get sick, of course you have insurance, but it wouldn't be better to have more buffer funds so that you do not have to sell your own personal assets. Your freedom fund can give you a peace of mind when health troubles start to come your way.

Insurance for the single breadwinner

To add to my previous point, say a household has a single breadwinner and the breadwinner gets sick, and is unable to work. If the family had a freedom fund in place, at least the income generated from the freedom fund can replace the breadwinner's income, in turn maintaining the standard of living for the whole family.

I've mentioned a lot about what your freedom fund can do for you. But remember, God did not allow you to have wealth just to fund your luxurious lifestyle. You will never truly be a champion of money if you do not utilise it to help your fellow men. If you hoard all the money you've earned for yourself, chances are, you'll never be able to experience the single greatest joy that anyone can feel, the joy of giving, being outrageously generous. And why? Why is it so counter intuitive that the greatest joy in the world is giving? Because when you give, you subconsciously show yourself and your brain that you don't live in a world of scarcity anymore, you live in a world of abundance, and when you feel the sense of abundance in your life, you'll never be slave to the feeling of lack any more. That's when you know you have truly attained the status of a money champion. God bless!

FINAL WORD

Money is sacred, don't let anyone tell you different. Don't be fooled by the saying that money is the root of all evil. It's not. It's the "love" of money, that is the root of all evil. People kill for money, people steal for money, why? Because they simply do not have it, and they become desperate because they can't support themselves and their families. Frankly, what I firmly believe in is, the lack of money is the root of all evil. I say this many times, ignorance is not bliss, ignorance is poverty, and I hate poverty, you should too. Sorry, let me rephrase. I HATE THE POVERTY MINDSET. Why? Because poverty leads to ruination and perdition. Poverty kills societies. Women and children are battered, and men resort to crime. Bad things happen to poverty-stricken neighbourhoods. It makes me sad to see people with narrow-minded, blocked mindsets about life and wealth, that they drive themselves towards poverty eventually, or at least, they work for 40 years of their lives and have nothing much to show for it at the end. Look, I'm not saying that I hate poor people, let me just put it out there. There are countries and peoples who are politically oppressed, hungry and without opportunity. They were unfortunately born in a place where they simply cannot get ahead and have no choice but to endure a harsh life. I get that. Don't you think that all the more we should find ways to help them? Wouldn't our purpose on earth be more meaningful then? The bulk of us who are probably reading this book would belong to the more fortunate bunch of people who have had good education, adequate food to eat and a roof over our heads. Chances are that people like us belong to the richest countries in the world. And yet, we take things for granted. Most of us have no goal, no vision, no discipline, and we mindlessly fill our homes and hearts with useless and meaningless material things. We "need" new clothes, we "need" to eat a steak dinner every night, we "need" Netflix. Ugh, this makes the Big Jodhi sick. Have some perspective please. We constantly take for granted the good things in life, and we squander our hard-earned money, while other people are so dirt poor they can't even afford to eat. It's time to have a change in our thinking and make the best out of the time we have on this earth.

Big Jodhi

INTRODUCTION: HOW TO ANALYSE REITS IN THE STOCK MARKET

D o you believe that you can own real estate for as little as 100 dollars? Welcome to the 3rd volume of "The Retail Investor" series. This volume will discuss about Real Estate Investment Trusts (REITs), what it is, how it works, how it runs and expands its business, and what you need to know to analyse a REIT like a pro.

Grow your money with REITs! Be a real estate mogul and build a steady stream of income through this wonderful investment vehicle!

May your days ahead be profitable and productive. Enjoy!

CHAPTER 1

Brick and Mortar

S helter. Everyone needs shelter. We use it for housing. We use it for schools. Entertainment. Storage. Manufacturing. Healthcare. Holidays. You name it. Ever since the dawn of Man, we have been building structures to host whatever activities we need to run our daily affairs. Houses, buildings, temples, and other forms of structures have been around for thousands of years! There is a great certainty that buildings and lands of sorts will be around in the years to come. It'll never lose its relevancy.

So, let's start with the term "real estate". The word "estate" means something that an individual owns that is of value. A person's estate essentially refers to his or her net worth. What comprises of estate? It can be stocks, bonds, mutual funds. It can be royalties. It can be a private business. Intellectual property rights. These assets are all part of an individual's estate. So, real estate means assets that are tangible and physical, hence the term "real estate". What is real estate? Buildings! Homes! Land. A physical structure or a piece of property built by men and used for shelter.

Many wealthy businessmen own real estate and properties of some sort in their portfolio. In fact, many tycoons make the bulk of their wealth through real estate. It never goes out of style, and any sophisticated investor and financially literate person can understand the power of real estate, and how it can generate a whole lot of wealth for the individual.

Let's explore an example:

Say you are a wealthy businessman with some spare change, 10 million dollars, and you found a nice shopping mall, named "Great Mall", within a residential enclave that is on sale. The tenancy is at almost 100% occupancy and the human traffic in that mall is impeccable. You decide to make an investment.

First, you check out the selling price of the mall. Uh oh. 20 million dollars. You're short of 10. Out of luck? Not at all! When it comes to real estate/ property investing, you have a strong ally, that ally is the bank. A bank will always be willing to loan an investor a sum of money to fund the purchase of a property. Why? Because the bank makes money by loaning money! Check it out.

Say the annual rental income from Great Mall is $800,000, and the bank is willing to loan you the $10 million (50% of the Great Mall's valuation) to fund the purchase, at an interest of 3% per annum. Let's do some maths here.

Yearly rental income from Great Mall: $800,000

Yearly interest from loan: 3% X $10 million = $300,000

Leftover income for the investor: $800k - $300k = $500k

The bank would pocket $300,000 in interest income from you, and you in turn would get to pocket the remaining $500,000 from the leftover income!

Now that the maths is done, you as the investor would need to judge the cash-on-cash return of your investment. So, you put in $10 million in this deal, and you earned $500,000 in residual cash flow, which calculates to a 5% cash-on-cash return. Not too shabby, considering that if you were to have the full 20 million dollars and dumped the whole amount into Great Mall, your cash-on-cash yield would only have been 4%.

As mentioned in the 2nd volume of "The Retail Investor" series, why real estate is such a great investment tool is that there is the additional aid of leverage. When you use borrowed money (debt) to fund your investments, you tend to augment your returns. This is why real estate investing is so powerful, you can grow your money a lot faster. However, do take caution that leverage is a double edged sword, if you are over extended on your debts, and you lose tenants in a recession, you're going to have to sell away your properties at distressed price and ultimately losing a boat load of your money and wealth. Ok, disclaimer aside, let's explore the capital appreciation segment of real estate investing.

Let's say Great Mall's valuation goes up by 10% in the next year, its new valuation will be $22 million, and you decide to cash out and sell. Let's check out the maths.

New valuation: $22 million

Repayment of loan: $10 million

Net proceeds from sale: $22 million - $10 million = $12 million.

Now, your cash-on-cash return is a solid 20% instead of 10%. Again this is the result of leverage, you augment your returns using debt to fund your property investment.

Owning a mall has many perks; the investment itself has a steady income stream, potential capital upside, and good protection against downside risks as well (huge number of tenants allows the building to be diversified in terms of rental income, unless all tenants move out at one go). Compared to buying a single home, it is more advantageous to own a property with multiple units. Single homes are for retail investors like us, and big buildings are for the big boys. Real estate moguls, wealthy businessmen and institutional investors. Boo Hoo. No chance for us? Not so fast. This is where a Real Estate Investment Trust (REIT) comes into play!

A REIT is a business, just like a stock, but simpler. When a REIT first starts out, it pools a sum of money from its initial investors (similar to an IPO process), and using this sum of money, the REIT purchases investment properties, of course with the help of the banks as well. Once this is all done, the REIT will eventually sell its shares into the stock market, and its units can be traded as stocks.

So, in Great Mall's case, say you as the investor would like to transform Great Mall into a REIT, Great Mall Retail Trust (GMRT), you would simply go through an IPO process and eventually sell shares of Great Mall Retail Trust into the secondary market, and, similar to the whole IPO eventuality, Great Mall Retail Trust will now have proceeds given by retail investors, to buy more buildings and expand. The retail investors and the initial owner then share the ups and downs of the REIT, along with the rental income that it provides. This is how a REIT works, in a nutshell. Let's explore how a REIT is beneficial to both the owner and the retail investors.

For the initial property owner

Unlocking capital for growth

Let's say that GMRT is publicly listed, and trading in the stock market. 60% of GMRT units belong to the public, 40% belong to you, the initial real estate investor. Because of the money that you have gained from the IPO process, you now have the proceeds to expand the REIT portfolio, but at the same time still maintaining ownership of the initial Great Mall that you had bought (not all but still a good chunk). You have unlocked precious capital from your investment property that you might have otherwise been stuck with, since the only way to get back capital for growth is to sell the Great Mall and buy a better mall that can provide higher returns. So, with a REIT structure, you have the flexibility to free up capital (by borrowing or using other people's money) to expand the REIT portfolio, at the same time still maintaining ownership of the previous properties that the property owner has bought.

The Great Mall example is fictional, albeit slightly similar to the real world. You see, the companies that start REITs are usually real estate developers. Real estate developers require a ton of capital to buy land from land banks, hire construction companies and architects, purchase raw material, and finally build the properties that they were intending to develop. Sometimes, they keep some of the buildings that they develop as an income producer, just to stabilise their business a little. They can only see the fruits of their labour once they sell off their whole inventory of units in their developments, which would take years if you include the construction duration, so earnings are rather erratic. Having a number of income producing buildings in their balance sheets would help to generate some income while they are waiting for their developments to finish construction. So, here's where the REITs would come in handy.

Since real estate developers are very capital-intensive businesses, they would need a substantial amount of capital should they spot a new opportunity for real estate development. So, how do they find capital? First, they borrow money the bank, or raise money through selling their short- or medium-term notes (kind of like short- or medium-term bonds). On top of that, they would create a REIT entity, and sell off those income producing buildings that they have on their balance sheets to the REIT that they have created, and use the remaining proceeds to fund their developments.

Still having a stake in properties sold off to REITs

Since it is the developers themselves that started up the REIT, they would have some ownership of the REIT, which also means that they still get to participate in the upside of the REIT and enjoy the income that it produces as well; in other words, by starting a REIT, the developers do not need to lose their full stake of the properties that they had intended to keep for income.

If you think about it, a REIT is like an ATM for a developer, because they can simply sell their buildings to the REIT to raise money. I'll explain how the REITs get money from the investors in my later chapters.

Tax advantages

REITs enjoy some tax benefits compared to a conventional company. If a developer were to hold on to its properties, the company would be taxed accordingly. However, if it were to spin off its properties into a REIT, the REIT will enjoy tax exemptions if they pay out at least 90% of their distributable income to its shareholders.

For the retail investor

Partying with the big boys

Well, where do I start? For us retailers, we get to participate in the real estate investing game that the big boys play! By big boys, I mean institutional investors and real estate companies. By being a single unit of a REIT, we get a small stake in their whole portfolio of properties, each with hundreds or even thousands of tenants. If we were just an average middle-class worker, the likelihood of us having enough savings to buy a whole building is pretty slim. With REITs being available to retail investors, we get to have a share of buildings worth tens of millions of dollars, may even billions.

Hands-off on property management

If we were just individual property investors, we would need to manage our tenants. A broken pipe, flickering lights, leaky roofs are to be handled by the landlords. On top of that, there will be tons of requests to entertain from tenants and extra maintenance services that we need to do as well. Rents are also collected by the landlord. All management duties for the investment property is handled by us, the landlord. However, with REITs, there is a management team to handle all the tenants and the overall maintenance of the building! They hire cleaners, provide for upkeep and maintenance, and collect the income on our behalf. As shareholders, our initial job was done the moment we handed over our hard-earned money to them at the IPO stage. They do the heavy lifting running the day to day operations for us.

Diversification

Imagine a shopping mall, or an office building. Say it has 4-10 stories, each floor with 5-10 tenants. Easily, we would have 20-100 tenants paying us rental income every month. Now, multiply that by 10, 20 or even 30, depending on the REIT that you buy, because most REITs have many buildings in their investment portfolio. The biggest REITs literally have thousands of buildings and properties. Pretty crazy right? You as the REIT investor would get to participate in the earnings of all those properties.

Liquidity

Imagine if you were to own a property, and suddenly you have a family emergency that requires money. If you did not have any back up funds in place, you would have to sell your assets to raise cash. If the property were to be your only asset, you would be in hot soup. Properties take weeks, sometimes even months to sell, you need to hire an agent to advertise, show prospective buyers around the house, and of course negotiate a reasonable price. Properties are rather illiquid, unless of course you're willing to let the property go at bargain basement prices. This would mean that you would very likely make a loss from the sale.

If you were to invest in REITs instead, the situation would be entirely different. See, a REIT is like a stock, it is publicly traded in the stock market, and the stock market is a very liquid platform. If you needed to raise cash, it would take you about 2-3 days to get your hands on the proceeds of the REITs that you sold off. As simple as that.

Low capital outlay

From my initial example on Great Mall, the capital outlay was $10 million. Let's scale it down a little. Say we as individual property investors were only looking for a small apartment to invest in, the little apartment would cost at least $50,000 to maybe as high as $800,000 to even $1,000,000, depending of course on the size and location of the apartment. I think it would take us a number of months or even years to save up that amount of capital, right? To make matters worse, we would only have one tenant; if the tenant leaves, there goes our income, and we would be stuck with the loan payments. The main disadvantage for investing on our own is that we need a heavy amount of capital, for a small number of tenants, most of the time it'll be just 1 to 3 tenants tops. With REITs, we can have as little as $50-$100 and we can already buy shares of the REIT; with that little amount of capital, we get exposure the numerous buildings and tenants that the REIT has! Which investment seems like the wiser choice? That one piece of real estate, or the single unit of REIT? Of course the REIT is a more suitable investment, as we can get into the real estate game faster, compared to saving up a few years to purchase a single property.

Of course, there is the argument that REITs charge very high management fees and as a REIT shareholder, and that we don't have control over the daily operations and business decisions, as compared to if we were to own a single property outright. Let's be realistic in this situation; until we generate so much wealth that we can buy a shopping mall or two on our own, the better choice would be to stick to REITs first.

CHAPTER 2

REIT Structure

L et's discuss about the REIT structure. So in the first chapter, we talked about how real estate developers initiates the start-up of a REIT. Any entity that starts up a REIT, or in finance speak, spins off its assets into a REIT, is called a sponsor.

Sponsor

The sponsor is the main beneficiary of the REIT since it would own a majority stake in it. The sponsor does not run the REIT itself; it is more like the supplier. The supplier of properties, and the sponsor sells its properties to the REIT. It also promotes the REIT.

In times of market downturns, the sponsor will be like a back-up plan, a goalkeeper you could say. It will help the REIT to tide through any financial difficulties it faces by providing funding, which is why a strong and stable sponsor is a key element when choosing a REIT to invest in. Of course, the REIT cannot always rely on the sponsor for financial support, it must grow on its own; it must be self-sustaining. So, how does it work towards self-sustenance? Through its REIT manager.

REIT manager

The REIT manager is in charge of the overall strategic direction of the company. To use the analogy of soccer, the REIT manager is the ace striker/ captain; the striker needs to score goals to win the game! And they double up as the captain, giving instructions to the lesser players. Similar to REITs, managers are usually seasoned veterans in the real estate game and are knowledgeable senior executives who know how to source for quality properties, with good anchor tenants and solid cash flow. They typically should have good relations with banks to get the best rates as well. REIT managers are critical in giving direction to the growth of the REIT.

Property Manager

The property manager is like the defender; they are in charge of running the daily operations of the REIT properties, and to ensure that all facilities are in running order, maintenance is prompt and tenants are happy. They are also executors of the instructions laid out by the REIT manager.

Trustee

The trustee is the referee. This trustee makes sure that all departments are in running order and no foul play is done under the table. In other words, the trustee acts on behalf of the interest of the shareholders of the REIT.

Shareholders

The shareholders are retail investors like you and me, and of course, institutional investors and the sponsor as well. We provide the initial funding, and we sit back and watch the cash fill our pockets and bank accounts. We do not control the daily operations of the company, but we can be part of important decision making through voting at company meetings (AGM or EOGM). This usually happens when a potential acquisition is in the pipeline, and the REIT manager needs the approval of the shareholders to go ahead with the acquisition.

CHAPTER 3

Types of REITs

Real estate can come in many forms. The most basic is of course a residential property, a studio apartment, or a private house where a family resides in. In the REIT world, there are many types of buildings and properties that have different uses.

Retail

This is a pretty common type of REIT, and you'll be able to do a ton of scuttle-butting to analyse these REITs. A retail REIT consists of shopping malls. They are usually situated around residential enclaves and they are the prettiest of the lot. I mean, when comparing with other types of REITs. Let me explain.

Ever visited a mall where everything is run down, toilets are dirty, and the paint is peeling off their walls? Some strip malls are so horribly maintained that they look like a scene from a zombie apocalypse movie.

Dust everywhere, the air conditioning is faulty and vacant units all around. Would you want to visit that mall again? Of course not!

Retail malls require human traffic, the REIT needs to attract people to visit the mall. So, they need to beautify the place to make shopping at the mall a pleasant experience. Toilets must be clean and dry, lights must be working, units must be brightly lit, and the overall ambience of the mall of must be welcoming. On top of that, retail malls need anchor tenants with a strong brand name, so that they can attract human traffic more effectively. This is what I mean by being the prettiest of the lot. Aesthetics play a huge part in the retail REIT game. Hence, on top of "peacocking", Retail REITs also conduct Asset Enhancement Initiatives (AEI) to keep the mall updated, current and fresh. This will add to the overall brand image of the mall, and, add to the valuation of the mall as well!

Retail REITs typically don't yield as much as other type of REITs, but what they can't deliver in distributions, they make it for with capital appreciation.

If they have strong anchor tenants that provide essentials for the population around them, you can bet your bottom dollar that the retail mall is a sustainable investment; and that the investment would be able to thrive in good times and survive in bad times.

Office

These bad boys portray an image of style, upper class, professionalism and posh. They are the second prettiest of the lot. Office REITs are usually located around the business districts of a country, and these buildings are leased by MNCs, banks, other financial institutions like insurance companies, accounting firms, law firms, and even government agencies.

Tenants of office REITs have to uphold a certain brand image, and they can and have to pay a premium to be located around the business districts areas. It would be strange for a global conglomerate headquarters to be located at a suburban strip mall, right? It just doesn't suit the brand.

Tenancies are also pretty long term as these businesses tend to stay put for the long term, so there is relatively stability in office REITs. There is also upside potential in valuations. Do take note, however, that they can be pretty cyclical in times of recessions. Companies may wind down on operations and there will be times when they close expensive offices in the business district areas just to cut down on some costs.

Industrial

Now this REIT is an ugly duckling. They may look like ducklings, but the industrial REIT is actually a cow. What type of cow? A cash cow. Industrial REITs provide logistical support for companies. They consist of storage facilities, warehouses, distribution centres and other industrial uses. As you know, the only people who visit these industrial buildings are the workers themselves. They do not require any flower-pots, nice fine dining areas, and clean walls to make the venue look attractive. They're all business. Of course, they can't be too run down, if not the workers will go bonkers eventually. More like, the main use of an industrial building is not to attract visitors. Rather, it is used to support companies with their logistical matters.

Amazon and Alibaba are now one of the biggest companies in the world. The E commerce scene has exploded over the past years, and it is changing the whole economic landscape of how we practice conventional retail. With E commerce, physical retail shops are starting to lose its usefulness as new business owners are venturing into online retail instead. There is less need for a physical storefront, or an outlet to store some inventory. Instead, warehouses and distribution centres are so much more in demand now, as E commerce grows. Inventory is stored in these warehouses and distribution centres, and finally sent off to their consumers.

Remember I said that industrial REITs were cash cows? They are the complete opposites of the retail REITs. Whatever upside that they lack in capital gains, they make it up for with distributions! The valuations of these industrial buildings rarely change, but the tenants are in the buildings for a pretty long time, and they pay good money to utilise the space for storage, industrial and logistical use. Hence, for an industrial REIT, the rental yield is significantly higher compared to an office or retail REIT. Investors who are more focused on cashflow can consider having a heavier weightage in industrial REITs.

If you pick the right industrial REIT with a strong tenant, chances are, they'll be able to weather financial storms as well. This ugly duckling, or, ugly cash cow, is really worth looking at.

Healthcare

If you're looking for stability, this is the REIT for you. Healthcare REITs consist of hospitals, nursing homes, hospices, specialist clinics, anything medical related. Demand for healthcare will most likely never go away; people get sick, people get old, and with aging population creeping slowly in developing countries, all the more will we experience a gradual increase in demand for healthcare REITs. In addition, with advances in medical technology and medical science, people tend to live longer as well.

Healthcare REITs are unique, because of the nature of the general healthcare industry, these medical facilities must be built in a way that the property can cater to the needs of its patients, hence it must be user friendly and safe for both the patients and the caregivers/ nurses.

Healthcare REITs are almost recession proof. Whether in good or bad economic seasons, healthcare is a must. Hence, having a good portion of your REIT portfolio diversified into healthcare will hedge against a downturn.

Hospitality

These babies are super cyclical. Hospitality REITs consists of hotels and resorts. During economic peaks, hospitality REITs often perform phenomenally well. They get revenue from tourists who stay in their hotels and resorts (Duh!). This particular REIT obviously does not have long term tenants; tourists stay for a few days and galivant to another holiday destination. Hospitality REITs use a particular metric called RevPAR (Revenue per available room) to benchmark their performance. The nature of a hospitality REIT's tenants is slightly different, and not necessarily bad, because on the plus side, tourists are ready to spend, and these hospitality REITs can make money through providing other services as well like serving meals, alcohol etc. Hospitality REITs tend to be priced extra high during an economic boom, so you might want to consider avoiding them till a recession comes.

Now, in recession times, do people spend more or less? Less! Do people travel more or less? Less! This is when the value of the hospitality REIT really gets hammered. Depending on the severity of the economic situation, if you do your research and conclude that the hospitality REIT that you're keen on buying can weather the impending financial storm, you can pick up some shares of these "holiday goodies" at dirt cheap prices, wait for the economy to turn back around and pocket a handsome profit. OR you can just hold the REIT altogether and sit on a tidy profit, while getting income from the REIT as well.

Diversified

Some REITS consist of not just one type of property. For instance, there are REITs that consist of both retail and office buildings. There are REITs that may even have a mixture of healthcare and retail! Why would REITs want to steer away from their "circle of competence", so to speak? Well, for diversification, obviously. Imagine if you owned a pure retail REIT, and a major recession hits, tenants can't keep up with rental payments and end up not renewing their lease. What then? Income is gone and the REIT share price plummets. There is potential for a pure play REIT to experience extreme volatility. However, if say the REIT that you bought was a diversified REIT that contained some industrial buildings, the income generated from the industrial buildings might offset the retail malls.

Diversified REITs are for investors who would like to attain a little bit of everything; balance is the name of the game here. Who knows how creative these REIT managers can get in time to come?

CHAPTER 4

REIT Risks

I know I know, I've been promoting too much about REITs, to a point where it seems like it's a sure-fire way to grow your money. Well, I wish it were so. Here are some pointers to take note of before investing in REITs.

Interest rate risk

We know that a REIT's capital structure is made up of equity and debt. In a nutshell, a REIT raises money from stakeholders, borrows money from banks, and use the proceeds to buy property and generate rental income. With that income, the REIT pays off the interest expense on the loan and the residual funds are distributed to the stakeholders.

Now, imagine a credit crunch, like in 2008. Credit markets froze, financial institutions were starved of money. Businesses couldn't function, wages could not be paid, inventory could not be bought. The economy was going through a financial meltdown. So, when the economy needs money, what does that mean? It means demand for money will increase. So, money has a price, right? What is its price? The price is: interest rate that banks charge to borrowers. What happens to interest rates when money is scarce? Interest rate charges increase. When interest rates increase, how will this affect REITS? Their interest expense goes up! More interest expense means less bottom-line profit, which in turn means less money distributed to shareholders! See how everything crumbles during a credit crunch? Scary.

Interest rate risk is not limited to just apocalypse type meltdowns. Generally, when inflation rises during economic booms, central banks around the world will raise general interest rates across the board to curb inflation, and when central banks increase interest rates, banks must follow suit. This may lead to the same effect of reduced income for REITs. Why? Because REITs need to refinance their loans every few years. With new loans at higher interest costs, REITs will have heavier expenses to settle, and less money to pay out to shareholders.

Liquidity risk

Similar to interest rate risk where we talked about the 2008 credit crunch, let me share with you how REIT loans work. Commercial property loans are slightly different from residential properties. For homestay, the mortgage lasts 25 to 30 years, and the homeowner slowly pays back interest to the bank and equity into the property. Commercial loans, however, don't last very long. They typically have a tenure of maybe 5-7 years, after which the borrower, in this case, the REIT, would require to make a balloon payment and return everything back. Now, as you know, REITs distribute 90% of their income, so how the heck is the REIT going to pay up? They don't. They refinance. In other words, they borrow money again from another bank to pay up to its previous bank, or they simply roll over the loans that they made with their current bank.

Now, during rosy times, everyone is happy, and money is freely sloshing back and forth around the economy. But what if the commercial loans mature at a time where there is a credit crunch? There is no way that a bank would roll over/ extend the loan. Instead, the bankers will politely tell the REIT," Hey REIT, you know what, we actually kind of need the cash now so we won't be able to extend the loan, so you need to pay us back." This will be detrimental to the REIT, because now they need to raise money, and they can only do it in limited ways, either dilute current shareholder value by doing a rights issue or preferential offering to raise money, or, sell off one of its buildings at a loss. Liquidity risk is real, and brutal to shareholders.

Concentration risk

Some REITs are exposed to concentration risk by having a majority of their revenue stream derived from just one property. Let's explore a hypothetical example.

Let's Great Mall Retail Trust (GMRT) grew from 1 property to 10 properties. Seems awesome right? The number of properties owned increased by tenfold. But what if 60% of the total rental income is coming from just 1 mall? What happens if say, a riot happens around that area and burns the mall to the ground (true story by the way). The REIT would lose 60% of its revenue!

Other than that, concentration risk can also come in the form of anchor tenants. If a REIT has a good chunk of its revenue from the same anchor tenant, the REIT is indirectly sharing its fate with the anchor tenant. If the anchor tenant goes bust, so does the REIT.

Foreign exchange (FX) risk

REITs do not limit their investments to their domiciled country, they often look for growth opportunities regionally as well. There are REITs that have become so globalised that their properties can be located in 5 or 6 countries, some even more. So, here comes another example. Let's say our fictional GMRT is a USD denominated REIT, and GMRT expands to Germany. Germany's currency is in EUR. So, during accounts reconciliation, the rental income in EUR must be converted to USD. If USD were to weaken against EUR, it would be favourable for GMRT, because the amount of euros collected in rental income can be exchanged for more USD; there is a gain in foreign exchange, leading to increased profits. However, if USD were to strengthen against the EUR, that means that same amount of euros collected in rental income can be exchanged for less USD, in turn leading to decreased profits. Some REITs may employ hedging tools in the event where they feel the currency that they are dealing with is volatile.

CHAPTER 5

Fund from operations

S tock valuations and performance metrics rely heavily on earnings; earnings show company growth, but not so much in the case of REITs. Let's address a fundamental issue on what deems a piece of real estate as valuable. Definitely a whole host of factors; location of building, age of building, tenants etc. But why do REIT managers focus on enhancing these qualities? What are they trying to achieve? All these qualities lead to a higher CASH-FLOW.

Residual cashflow from the REIT is mainly what shareholders want, and it is also why REITs got started in the first place. REITs were meant to give the public a chance to earn cash from good and diversified real estate. In addition, the growth part comes mainly from investing opportunities, spotting good buys from quality real estate, not so much on improving business processes to grow the business. Once the investment property is purchased, the income and cashflow is pretty much passive from there.

So, when analysing a REIT, look at how much fund from operations (FFO) the REIT is generating. This metric shows pretty much the raw rental income.

Let's use the income statement from our fictional REIT, GMRT. And oh, let's imagine that they have grown quite substantially from the last time we talked about GMRT.

GMRT
Income Statement

	'000
Revenue	$315,000
Property Expenses	$63,000
Other Expenses	
Trustee fees	$5,000
Management fees	$25,000
General and Administrative	$15,000
Interest	$27,000
Depreciation and Amortisation	$90,000
Other Income	
Gain on sale of property	$10,000
Net Income	**$100,000**

Revenue represents gross rental income. As you can see from the image, it is the top line item, sitting at $315 million. Then we net off all other expenses and add the gain on sale of property to get the net income of $100 million. Now, how do we find the FFO from here? We need to think about cash. Which line item(s) in the income statement is not a cash expense? I'll give you 3 seconds to think about the answer. 1 Mississippi, 2 Mississippi, 3 Mississippi.

I hope you guessed it right. The answer is depreciation and amortisation expense. If you didn't guess it right, I highly suggest you read the 1st volume of "The Retail Investor" series. Depreciation and amortisation does not take cash out of the business during the fiscal year, and it is more of an accounting rule that every business must adhere to, I won't go into the details of this.

So, we have our net income of $100 million, and we have $90 million in D & A expense. We simply add the two together to get the total cash collected for the year.

$100 million + $90 million = $190 million.

Before we say "Bingo!", ask yourself if this is truly the FFO.

Let's think about the purpose of finding out the FFO of a REIT. It is to measure what their regular income is, in turn analysing the sustainability and earning power of its properties. Now, if you look closely at the 2nd last line item of the income statement, we see the gain on sale of property of $10 million. Ask yourself this: how often do REITs actually sell off their investment properties, and should we include it as a part of their regular business model?

The answer is a firm no. Divestments in properties do not occur all the time, and it all depends on the current market situation and valuation levels of real estate. If REITs were to continuously sell off properties every year, whether in good or bad years, they can potentially lose money and earning power. Hence, we need to subtract off the gain on sale of property to get the FFO.

Here we go.

$190 million - $10 million = $180 million.

Now, this is the true FFO. Let's say GMRT has 100 million shares outstanding, their FFO per share will be:

$$\frac{\$100m + \$90m - \$10m}{100m} = \$1.80 \; per \; share$$

To sum up, the formula for calculating FFO/ share is:

$$FFO \; per \; share = \frac{\text{Net income} + \text{Depreciation \& Amortisation} - \text{Gain on sale of property}}{\text{Shares outstanding}}$$

CHAPTER 6

REIT metrics

I nvestors love metrics. Metrics give guidance to whether an asset is worth investing in. Take for example: key performance metrics, where employees get appraised based on KPI as they indicate whether employee performance is good or bad, and whether the employee has brought value to the company or not. Same with investment metrics, they show whether an investment can bring value to the investor or not. Let's look at some REITs metrics that can be useful for your REIT research.

*Disclaimer: Do not use any of these ratios as a single metric to determine your investment decisions (it is not 100% guaranteed that you will make money just from using this ratio) as you can potentially lose all your capital if you do not do additional in depth research and critical thinking on the prospective REIT's fundamentals.

Capitalisation rate

Let's utilise our first financial metric for REITs, the capitalisation rate, or cap rate. The cap rate measures the yield of cashflow from the purchase price of the REIT.

Using GMRT's example, let's say GMRT is selling at $8.50 per share in the stock market. We have already analysed in the previous chapter that the FFO is $1.80 per share. So, we simply take the FFO divided by the share price.

$$Capitalisation\ rate = \frac{FFO\ per\ share}{Share\ price}$$

GMRT's cap rate is 1.80 divided by 8.50, which would give us a 21% cap rate, a very high cap rate in fact. Of course, when you're making a purchase decision, you can come up with your own set of rules on what the minimum cap rate you would demand from your own REIT investments.

One thing to take note, the fund from operations do not mean that investors get paid that full amount, it just shows the fundamental earning power of the whole REIT on a regular basis. The amount of money that investors get paid is called the distribution yield.

Distribution yield

The distribution yield is similar dividend yield for

stocks. It is the amount of money that a REIT pays out to shareholders. For stocks, the board of directors and management committee decide on the amount of dividends to pay out. REITs, on the other hand, are required to pay out at least 90% of their income to shareholders. Let's illustrate this with an example.

From the income statement in the previous chapter, we see that GMRT's net income is $100 million, so, GMRT is required to pay out $90 million (90% of net income). Assuming that GMRT has 100 million shares outstanding, and that their share price is at $8.50 per share, the distribution yield would be:

$$Distribution\ yield = \frac{Distribution\ per\ share}{Share\ price}$$

Distribution per share: $90 million ÷ 100 million shares = $0.90 per share

Share price: $8.50

Distribution yield = $0.9 ÷ $8.50 = 10.5%

This is considered a pretty high yield! Investors would typically get this type of distribution yield during very oversold markets. So, relating back to the retail investor, if you had invested $100,000 in GMRT, you would be getting $10,500 in cold hard by the end of the year, which equates to $875 per month. Do about 2 to 3 more of these type of purchases and you would be yielding at least $2,000 worth of distributions per month. Financial freedom here we come.

Weighted average debt tenure (WADT)

The weighted average debt tenure measures the average time needed before a REIT needs to refinance. The shorter the WADT, the more urgent the REIT would need financing. During boom times, people may overlook this metric because money is easily available. However, please beware that a REIT with a short WADT does not get caught in a liquidity crisis (as explained earlier in the chapter about risks). Let's explore how WADT is calculated.

Let's assume that GMRT has a number of loan obligations.

Borrowings	Maturity
$300 million	2 years
$200 million	2 years
$900 million	5 years
$100 million	3 years

Now, they have a total of 1.5 billion dollars in total borrowings, with each loan maturing at a different time. It would be difficult for investors to analyse how significant each loan obligation is, relative

THE RETAIL INVESTOR 3 BOOKS IN 1

to the whole portfolio and overall capital structure of the REIT. This is where the WADT evens out the comparison, by giving each loan obligation a certain weightage.

Multiply each maturity duration by a percentage of its loan amount relative to the total amount of borrowings.

Borrowings	Weightage	Maturity	Weighted Maturity
$300 million	20%	2 years	0.4
$200 million	13%	2 years	0.26
$900 million	60%	5 years	3
$100 million	7%	3 years	0.21

The weightage column represents the percentage of that particular loan obligation relative the whole loan amount that GMRT has outstanding. (300 million is 20% of 1.5 billion).

After we get the weighted maturity values of all the individual loan obligations, we simply add all the values up.

Weighted average tenure of debt

= 0.4 + 0.26 + 3 + 0.21 = 3.87 years.

With this metric, we can say that the average debt maturity of all of GMRT's borrowings is 3.87 years.

Average cost of debt

This metric will show the overall interest cost relative to the total amount of borrowings. The lower the percentage, the cheaper the debt is, which also means that the REIT is effective in getting the best rates. Let's look at GMRT's borrowings again.

Borrowings	Interest rate	Interest expense
$300,000,000	2.5%	$7,500,000
$200,000,000	3.5%	$7,000,000
$900,000,000	1.0%	$9,000,000
$100,000,000	3.5%	$3,500,000

We will add up all the interest expense together and divide the total interest expense by total borrowings.

Total borrowings: $1.5 billion

Total interest expense: $7.5 million + $7 million + $9 million + $3.5 million = $27 million

Average cost of debt = $27 million ÷ $1.5 billion = 1.8%

That's a dirt-cheap interest rate. I would like to remind you that GMRT is a fictional REIT, in a fictional Eutopia where money is available all the time and the economy is in a perpetual state of progress and prosperity (I kid).

Weighted average lease expiry (WALE)

Malls are filled with hundreds of tenants, each of them with a lease contract. Every now and then, an existing tenant lease expires or gets renewed, maybe new tenants come in and get new lease contracts. All these tenants with different lease durations can be combined into a single metric to determine, on average, how long a tenant rents a unit in a particular property.

For simplicity's sake, let's imagine that there are 5 main tenants in GMRT. There will also be a breakdown of how much rental income each tenant contributes.

Tenants	Rent contribution	Lease expiry (years)
Tenant A	$15,000,000	4
Tenant B	$112,000,000	5
Tenant C	$45,000,000	4
Tenant D	$123,000,000	2
Tenant E	$20,000,000	3

Similar to WADT, a weightage is given for each tenant, based on the percentage of their rental income relative to total revenue.

Tenants	Rent contribution	Lease expiry (years)	Weighted expiry
Tenant A	$15,000,000	4	0.19
Tenant B	$112,000,000	5	1.78
Tenant C	$45,000,000	4	0.57
Tenant D	$123,000,000	2	0.78
Tenant E	$20,000,000	3	0.19

Add up the sum of all the weighted expiries, and you get the WALE of GMRT.

WALE: 0.19 + 1.78 + 0.57 + 0.78 + 0.19 = 3.51 years.

This metric shows that the average tenant has about 3.51 years before his or her lease expires, which would in turn show the investor how long the income can last before the GMRT needs to hustle for more tenants or renew lease contracts. A low WALE is a disadvantage for a REIT.

Gearing

This is a crucial metric. How can we tell if a REIT is conservatively financed? Since we know that REITs cannot keep a lot of cash reserves for rainy days, we must be very strict in judging the prudence of a REIT. We can do this by using the gearing ratio.

Let's imagine that the total value of all of GMRT's properties is $4 billion. From the previous sections of this chapter, we know that GMRT's total amount of borrowings add up to $1.5 billion. So, to calculate gearing ratio, we divide the total amount of borrowings with the total value of GMRT's properties, in other words, total assets.

$$Gearing\ Ratio = \frac{Total\ debt}{Total\ assets}$$

Total debt: $1.5 billion

Total assets (total value of GMRT's properties): $4 billion

Gearing ratio: $1.5 billion ÷ $4 billion = 37.5%

This gearing ratio is considered reasonably conservative. Typically, REITs can go as high as 40 or even 50% gearing.

Now, let me enlighten you on why this is so important. Banks loan money based on the value of a property. For instance, in GMRT's case, the bank loans a billion dollars with a caveat, that the total loan amount cannot be greater than 50% of the total value of the properties owned by GMRT. We know that property valuations fluctuate, right? So in booming markets, say the value of GMRT's properties increase to $10 billion, that would make the loan amount of $1.5 billion just 15% of the total value of GMRT's properties. Still ok. But, if say a recession hits, and GMRT's properties' total value drops to $1.8 billion (killer bear market), the loan amount of $1.5 billion is now 83% of the GMRT's total property value! The bank would go to GMRT and say, "Hey GMRT, you've failed to hit the minimum valuation requirement, so you need to top up money with us to go back to the minimum 50% requirement, if not we'll foreclose on your properties. Now pay up!" Scary, isn't it? This is why a conservative gearing ratio is so important for investors to insist on. Yes, it means less yield, but it also means protection of capital.

Having a conservative gearing ratio does not always mean defensive; if a REIT has a low gearing ratio at the right time (economic boom), they would actually be in a perfect position to expand. Why? Because of debt headroom. REITs have a cap on the amount of gearing they can have, usually   at 50%. So, if say GMRT was at this particular gearing ratio of 37.5% during say the start of a new economic cycle, they effectively have another 12.5% debt headroom to buy more properties!

Gearing ratio is an absolute must when analysing REITs and making a REIT investment, so please read this segment again if you need to.

Interest Cover Ratio

Another metric to use for judging the prudence of a REIT is the interest cover ratio. This metric will tell you if a REIT's interest expense is manageable. You may ask, why do we need a metric like this to see if a REIT is conservative? Isn't it common sense that the higher the gearing, the higher the interest expense, right? Not so. We must remember that in every economic cycle, interest rates vary. If a REIT has a high gearing ratio during periods of low interest, they can probably keep up with loan obligations.

So, how do tell if they can keep up with their loan obligations and interest expenses? By comparing their net income with interest expense. Simply divide the net income by total interest expense. Let's use GMRT as an example.

$$Interest\ cover\ Ratio = \frac{Net\ income}{Interest\ expense}$$

Net income: $100 million

Interest expense: $27 million

Interest cover ratio: $100 million ÷ $27 million = 3.7 times.

Typically, a REIT with about a 5-interest cover ratio is considered pretty safe. Some really solid REITs can even go up to 7-9 times. Not so for GMRT's case. Ouch. 3.7 is actually a pretty dangerous number for an interest cover ratio. This value of 3.7 means that GMRT's net income 3.7 times the amount of interest expense, if revenues were to drop, GMRT may have trouble servicing the loans and interest payments.

Do you see now, why pairing both the gearing and interest cover ratio is so important? Just using either one of these metrics is not sufficient to judge the prudence of a REIT, both metrics must be used hand in hand, and if either one of these 2 metrics don't meet your investment criteria, don't buy the REIT. Period.

CHAPTER 7

Raising capital for growth

L et's talk about how REITs grow their property portfolio. As you know, REITs use debt to fund their purchases. However, it can't be a 100% debt purchase, banks would seldom or never loan out to a business venture without having the investor have at least some skin in the game. So, every investment property purchase must have a mixture of debt, and the REIT's own money, or, equity, we call it. Where is the REIT going to get its own money from? REITs pay out 90% of their income every year! That meagre 10% is used for cash reserves in case they need to fund additional operational duties. The remaining cash won't be sufficient to fund any investment opportunities. This is where the stakeholders come into play.

REITs very often conduct private and public offerings to their stakeholders; they create and sell more shares to their stakeholders, sometimes non-stakeholders as well, at discounted prices, to raise money. Let's use GMRT as an example.

Say GMRT found a great retail mall valued at $100 million and they would like to buy the building. So, they go to a bank and say, "Hey bank, loan me some money, I've a got a great deal on a property." The bank says, "sure I'll loan you some money, I'll fund 30% of the deal." Ouch, that's a low percentage, but GMRT agrees, nevertheless. So, the bank disburses a grand total of $30 million to GMRT.

Now, GMRT needs to figure out where to get the remaining $70 million. Easy. Use public money. GMRT can set a discounted price that they would like to sell their additional shares at, and raise the money required. Let's do up some sums and projections.

Say GMRT feels that they can raise money by selling at $7 per share (an almost 20% discount to the current market price of $8.50), they can organise a public or private offering of additional 10 million shares to sell, $7 a pop. This will allow them to get the funding they need for the purchase. 3 main types of offerings that REITs conduct.

Preferential offering

This type of offering is for stakeholders only. So, if GMRT were to conduct a preferential offering, they would allow only existing stakeholders to buy, and also with certain criteria, say, for every 2 shares that a stakeholder owns, he or she is allowed to buy 1 additional share at $7. Let me elaborate with an example.

A retail investor owns 100 shares, so he or she is allowed to purchase 50 additional shares at $7 each. Total amount of money that the retail investor would have to come up with is 50 x $7 = $350 to pay for the shares and ultimately to the REIT.

A preferential offering is non renounceable, which means that if an existing stakeholder does not want to participate in the preferential offering exercise, he or she would not be able to give or sell off that "right" to buy the discounted shares to anybody else.

Rights issue

This is a very similar type of public offering to the preferential offering option. The only difference is that, if a stakeholder does not want to participate in the rights issue, he or she has the choice to sell the rights over to anybody else who wants to buy them; usually this can be done easily through a broker. So, the whole initial process of raising capital and buying discounted shares stay the same, apart from the choice given to the stakeholder on whether he or she wants to sell the rights.

Private placement

This is a private offering given to institutional and accredited investors. The primary reason for conducting a private placement is speed; when a great opportunity arises and a deal needs to be closed fast, a REIT would go to entities and people that they know have the money to foot the bill. This is unlike the public offerings, where the whole exercise can take weeks to complete, so the monies are raised at a slower pace, often not timely enough to secure a great property deal.

Implications to shareholders

Public offerings are great because they allow stakeholders to increase their holdings in the REIT itself; if the REIT is well run, stakeholders get more upside on the growth of the REIT, since they can own more shares, and at a discount too! However, there is a downside. When a stakeholder chooses not to participate/buy the additional shares in the offering, the stakeholders will experience a dilution in the value of their holdings with the REIT. Let's use GMRT as an example.

Say stakeholder A owns 10 million shares of GMRT before the public offering, that works up to owning 10% of GMRT (10 million ÷ 100 million shares outstanding).

After the public offering exercise, the new shares outstanding will be 100 million + 10 million = 110 million shares outstanding. If stakeholder A were to give up his rights, or choose not to participate in the preferential offering, then stakeholder A's new vested interest in GMRT will be 9% (10 million ÷ 110 million shares outstanding), he or she would have lost 1% stake in GMRT. This would in turn lead to less claim over the income generated by the REIT, and ultimately less value compared to the other stakeholders.

This is even more so for private placements. Private offerings are only available to the big boys, so the retail stakeholders do not even get a chance to participate in the private placement, the dilution is automatic.

Having said all that, dilution is painful in the near term, but, if the REIT can use the money well and increase even more profits over time, then either way all stakeholders will benefit regardless.

Advantages of having a good sponsor

Another silver lining to this is that if the REIT's sponsor is an established developer who builds great properties, the REIT can have a right of first refusal (ROFR) over all of the sponsor's income producing properties should the sponsor want to sell off a building. In other words, the REIT calls dibs on the sponsor's quality properties.

CHAPTER 8

Red flags

Congratulations on reaching the last chapter of this book. We have been discussing mostly good stuff about REITs. Let me leave you with some precautions on how to spot a bad REIT.

Beware of high yields

Don't be hasty in buying a REIT with an absurdly high yield. Remember that distribution yields are compared using past data, you never know if the next quarter will be the same. Chances are, if you see that a REIT is paying a very high distribution yield, it will likely mean that their stock price has been hammered down due to negative events specific to the REIT. It can be issues like a major tenant not renewing a lease, or a riot, or a bribery case or a scandal of some sort. Always check back to more than just one year of data, compare past year's earnings, FFOs, and distribution amounts to analyse the growth story of the REIT. Of course, have a general understanding of their underlying properties as well.

The only exception to this is when the whole market is experiencing a correction, or when a bear market has come. This is usually the time where everything is sold off, both good and bad stocks. So, if the economy is in a recession and stock prices are low, you will more often than not see very high yields on stable companies, including REITs. This is the time where you heave whatever savings you have into these bad boys (I mean quality REITs) and reap a great harvest in the future years to come.

Credit Rating

REITs often get credit rating scores from the 3 main credit rating agencies, Standard & Poor's, Moody's, and Fitch. The credit rating agencies set a bunch of balance sheet and earnings criteria for different categories of credit ratings, like triple A, double B, triple B, or even junk ratings. Avoid REITs with a bad credit rating label. REITs with a good credit rating would often get better interest rate deals from banks as well, since they are seen as less risky and more stable, banks are willing to loan good quality REITs with more money and less interest. Win-win situation for both the bank and the REIT.

Yield accretive acquisitions

Take note that when a REIT is doing an investment,

the outcome must eventually be that the distributions be higher than before the acquisition itself. There may be some purchases that cause distributions to be lower. You might be wondering, how D.U.M.B can the REIT management be to purchase a property that would lower the overall income of the REIT. Well, sometimes, investments can have more strategic value than just tangible near term monetary gains, so once again, please do your research to see where the REIT management is coming from when they are doing an investment and find out exactly what their reason is for deciding to make such an investment.

Income support

For freshly minted REITs, sometimes they experience an initial bout of empty units in their properties since they are new. On top of that, the REIT would need to attract funding to grow, how the heck are they going to attract funding early in the game when they do not even have rental income to show investors that they are worth investing in? This is again where the sponsor comes in. A strong sponsor will provide income support to a new REIT for the first few years, just to tide them over the beginning stages. It's like a father giving an initial sum of money to his son when he first becomes an adult. The new REIT will have a benchmark income to aim for, say $50 million in income must be generated every year. So, they would take the first few years to hustle for new tenants. In the meantime, whatever shortfall that they have, the sponsor will top up for them. If say for the first year, a new REIT only generated $40 million in income, the sponsor will support the income by paying an additional $10 million to the REIT.

Now, take note that this only lasts for a few years. Once the support period ends, the income support ends as well. If the REIT fails to hit a sustainable benchmark income by the time the support period ends, the net income will experience a sudden drop, along with the distributions, and ultimately the stock price as well. Boo Hoo. Buyer beware.

FINAL WORD

I hope that book has given you a better insight on how REITs work. More importantly, I hope this book inspires you to learn even more about REITs! Don't stop at The Retail Investor. There are tons of other books and material that can really equip you to be a well-informed investor, so that you can ultimately make great investments to grow your wealth. The real estate game has been made much easier to participate since Congress approved of REITs in the 1960s. Capitalise on it! Won't you want a steady stream of income for the rest of your days?

I'm on a crusade. I'm speaking up for the little guys, like spider-man. Friendly neighbourhood Retail Investor. More than just about REITs, I hope that my books have given you confidence to take charge of your financial destiny, and that there is a way to solidify your financial independence, through investing in the stock market. Read up, study hard, equip yourself with knowledge, be bold and take the plunge. It would be the best decision of your life. Of course, don't dump all your money in one stock. Be careful about it too, these methods that I have share can aid you in making good purchases, not guaranteed of course, but it will definitely increase your chances of making money like a pro in the stock market.

May your days ahead be profitable and productive. God bless!

Big Jodhi

ABOUT THE AUTHOR

Big Jodhi

Big Jodhi is just an Average Joe who loves reading about money and thinking about money in his spare time. He loves stories about capitalism and his heroes include Cornelius Vanderbilt, JP Morgan, Jay Gould, Benjamin Graham, John Templeton, Warren Buffet, Peter Lynch, Walter Schloss, Seth Klarman, Mohnish Pabrai, Kevin O'Leary, Howard Marks, Sam Walton, Lee Ka-Shing, Robert Kuok, Mochtar Riady and Joel Greenblatt.